Vintage Women

ADULT COLORING BOOK #1

FEATURING 42 PAGES OF CLASSIC ART BY NELL BRINKLEY

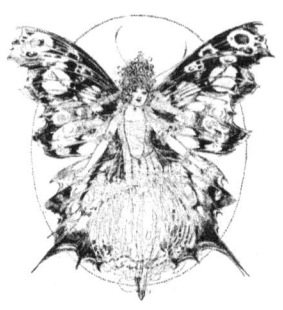

FROM THE EDITORS OF CLICK AMERICANA®
CLICKAMERICANA.COM

INTRODUCTION BY NANCY J. PRICE
EDITOR-IN-CHIEF, MYRIA.COM & AUTHOR OF "DREAM OF TIME"

Vintage Women: Adult Coloring Book #1
Classic Art by Nell Brinkley

Copyright © 2015 by Synchronista LLC and Nancy J Price

This book features digitally-edited and restored versions of selected illustrations by Nell Brinkley (1886 – 1944). While the originals are now in the public domain, this book collection, format and all copyrights to those derivative works are reserved by Synchronista LLC, and the images herein may not be reproduced without express written permission.

Original images provided courtesy of the US Library of Congress

Synchronista® and Click Americana®
are registered trademarks of Synchronista LLC

Published by Synchronista LLC – Gilbert, Arizona, USA

www.Synchronista.com

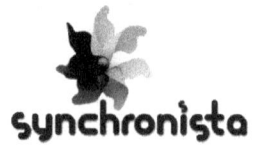

Introduction

More than a century ago, a young artist named Nell Brinkley picked up a pen... and drew her way into history.

The girl had natural talent. Just a couple of decades after her arrival on this planet, the young Miss Brinkley's iconic black and white line art began to regularly appear in newspapers across the United States.

In contrast to the staid, serene "Gibson Girls" that had been popular for many years, Brinkley's illustrations were a breath of fresh air. The women she depicted were vibrant and vivacious, relatable and real, independent and inspiring — and were embraced by the public almost immediately.

Despite her unique style making her a household name, the majority of her individual works were quickly relegated to dusty archives, and all but lost to later generations. (In fact, I only happened upon Brinkley's art by accident, while seeking historical treasures for the ClickAmericana.com website.)

While her most common theme was the pursuit of love — with wistful and playful overtones by turn — she also portrayed motherhood, recreational pastimes, daily life... plus enjoyed taking the occasional fanciful departure.

The collection in this book, however, focuses primarily on the on the everyday girls and women she so gracefully depicted, and showcases more than three dozen of Brinkley's works created between 1912 and 1919.

Now you can enjoy a little modern-day relaxation and the chance to explore your creativity while giving these enchanting drawings from the past a whole new life.

More than just something new for you to color, these illustrations capture moments in time, and as such, offer tiny glimpses into life a hundred years ago — moments that had been forgotten for decades. Every page offers something different — and maybe even a little bit magical, and will make for beautiful keepsakes to frame or share.

Hope you love them as much as I do!

Best,

Nancy J. Price
Founder, Click Americana
Editor-in-Chief, Myria.com
Author, *Dream of Time*

Important notes

When Nell Brinkley first put pen to paper, she probably never imagined her work would be seen and appreciated more than a hundred years later.
But her artistic flair is just one of many things that make this book unique.

Within these covers, dozens of Nell Brinkley's lifestyle portraits of women have been rediscovered and transformed into coloring pages. Every one of the antique images in this book was carefully chosen, then painstakingly restored by hand using modern technology in order to return it to its original glory as much as possible.

Before creating this collection, we reached out to coloring book fans, and incorporated as many of their suggestions as we could:

- Each highly-detailed antique picture is printed only on one side of the paper, allowing you to color with your choice of medium without worrying about bleed-through to an image on the back. (If you like, slip a blank page from the end of the book behind the picture you're coloring to avoid ink or paint bleeding onto the next illustration.)
- Page numbering, titles and other image information appears on the reverse of each page, ensuring the coloring side is distraction-free and could be suitable for framing.
- Illustrations with a portrait orientation start the book, while landscape images are grouped in the second half.

Although Brinkley's pictures were not created with colored pens, pencils, crayons or paints in mind, we reviewed hundreds of drawings to select those most suited to the task. Still, due to the authentic vintage nature of the artwork, this isn't a typical adult coloring book of modern images with pristine lines.

The images were restored as faithfully as possible, but since the original artwork is not known to exist, we relied upon high-resolution scans of the printed newspaper pages. As such, there are a few caveats:

- Borders, shapes and lines are occasionally incomplete.
- Some details have been lost due to printing processes and quality of preserved newsprint.

In addition, in keeping with the artist's original designs, you will also see...

- The pictures are often very intricate.
- There are large areas of black on certain pages.
- There's an overall sketch-like quality on some illustrations, particularly near the edges.
- We chose not to over-simplify the artwork because of the tremendous amount of detail (and personality) that would be lost in the process.

We hope these hand-drawn snapshots of history in the making inspire your muse — and we would love to see how you bring color to these beautiful vintage women! You're invited to post your creations on the book's Amazon.com page, or the Synchronista page at facebook.com/synchronista. Thank you!

Welcome!

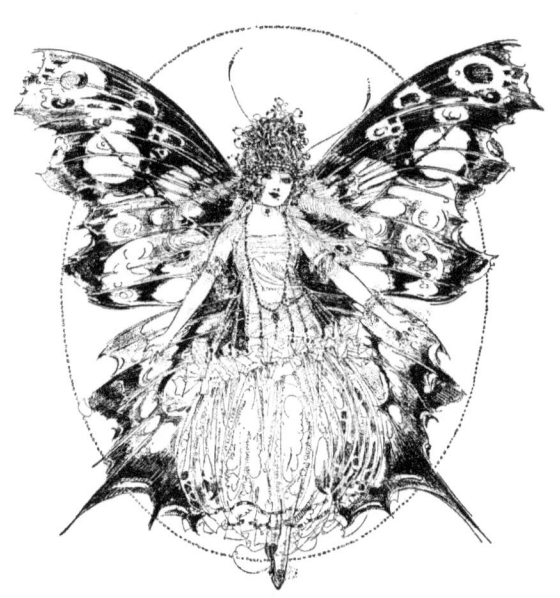

"I would rather... have had the grass and the flowers and the sunshine — the bubbles of tender color called dreams — the space of perfect youth and idle, blind play — than not, my friend."

~ Nell Brinkley, *Love and Death* (1913)

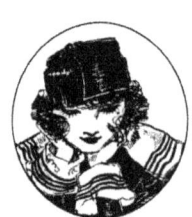

*Tip: Find the details about the
following illustrations in this
space on the back of each page.*

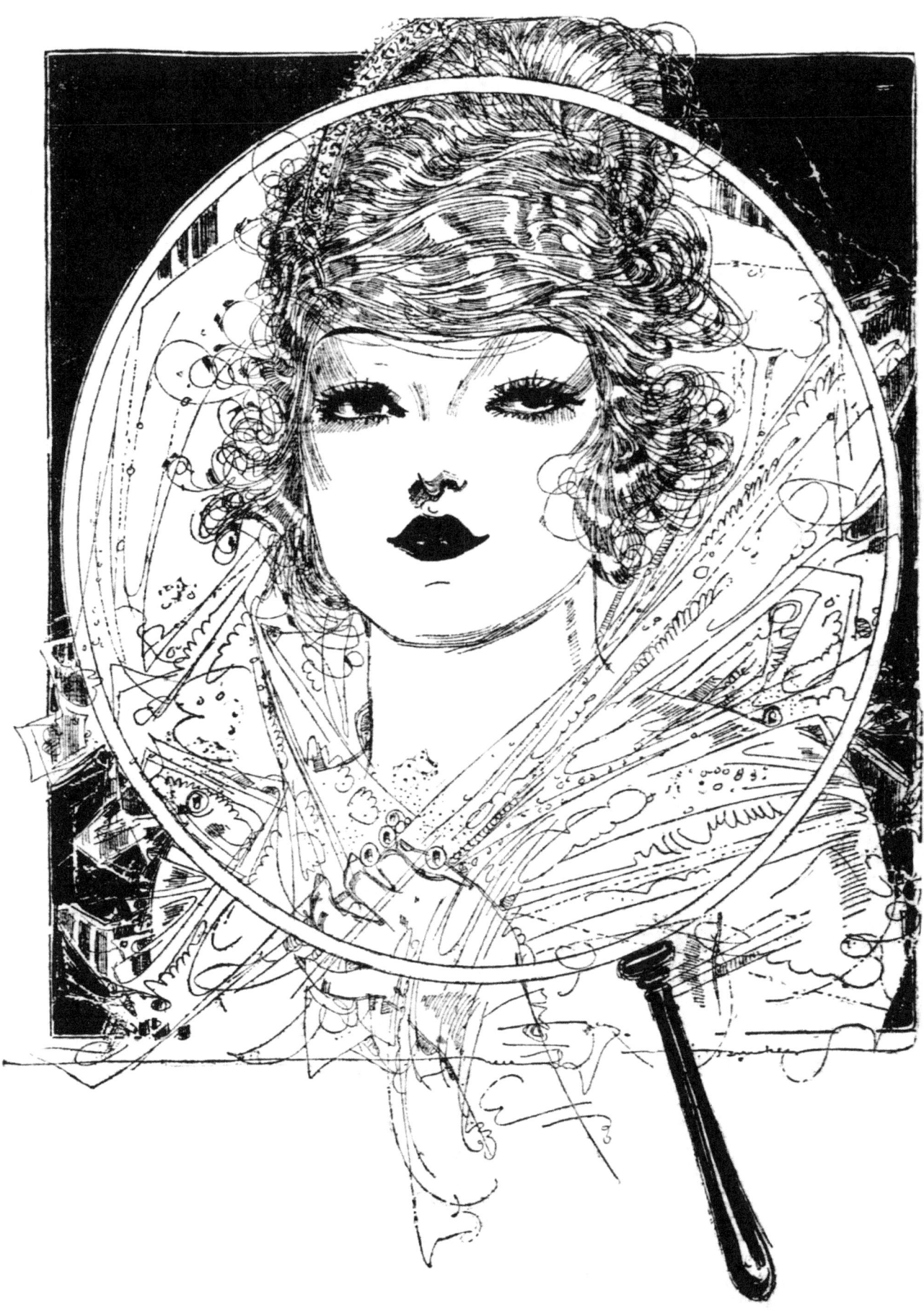

ABOUT THE ILLUSTRATION ON THE REVERSE

Original publication: Omaha Daily Bee (Nebraska)

Publication date: June 07, 1915

Title: "Germ of a Fatal Heart Trouble"

Artist: Nell Brinkley

© Copyright 2015 by Synchronista LLC & ClickAmericana.com

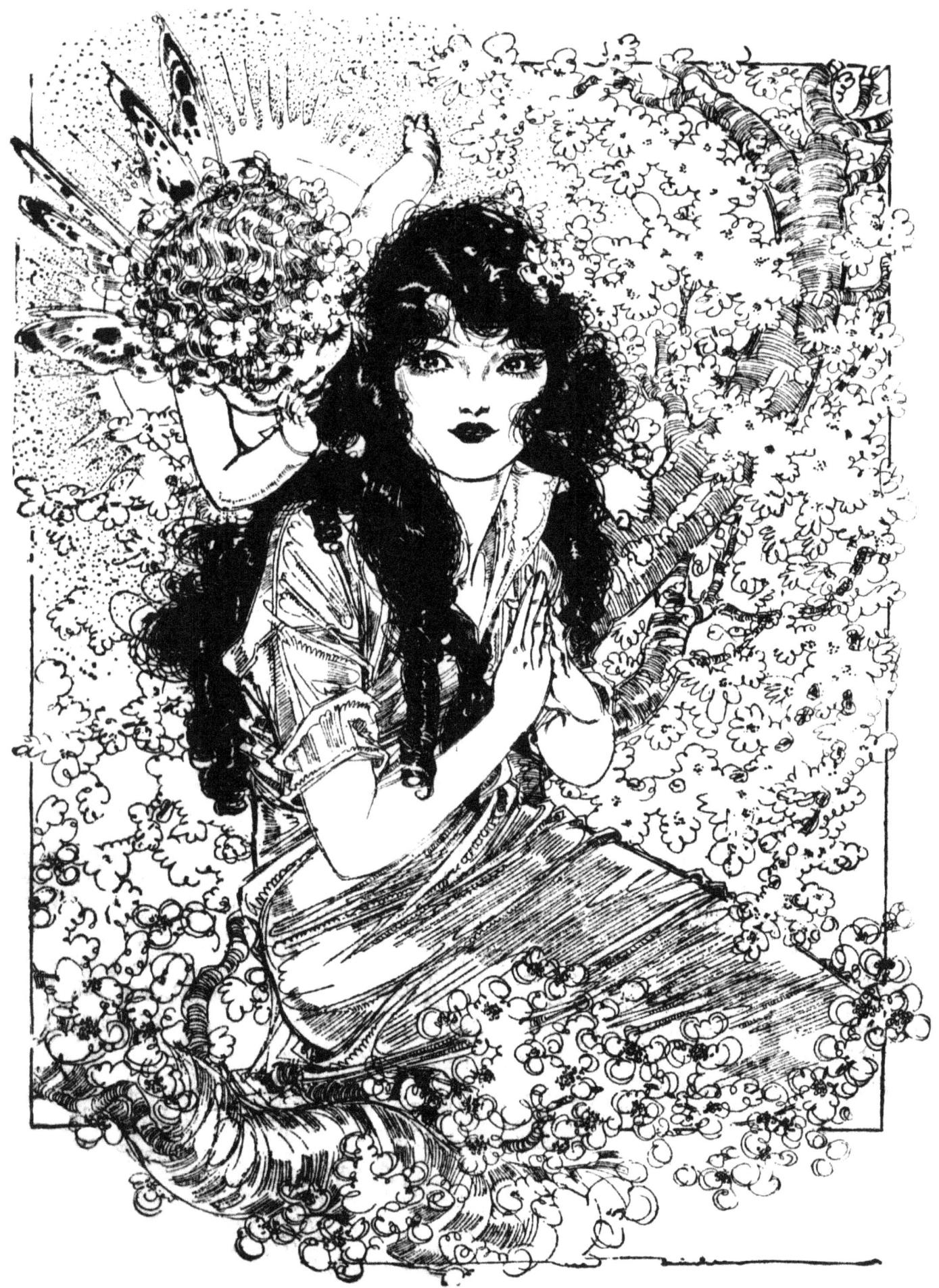

ABOUT THE ILLUSTRATION ON THE REVERSE

Original publication: Omaha Daily Bee (Nebraska)
Publication date: March 29, 1915
Title: "The First Whisper"
Artist: Nell Brinkley

© Copyright 2015 by Synchronista LLC & ClickAmericana.com

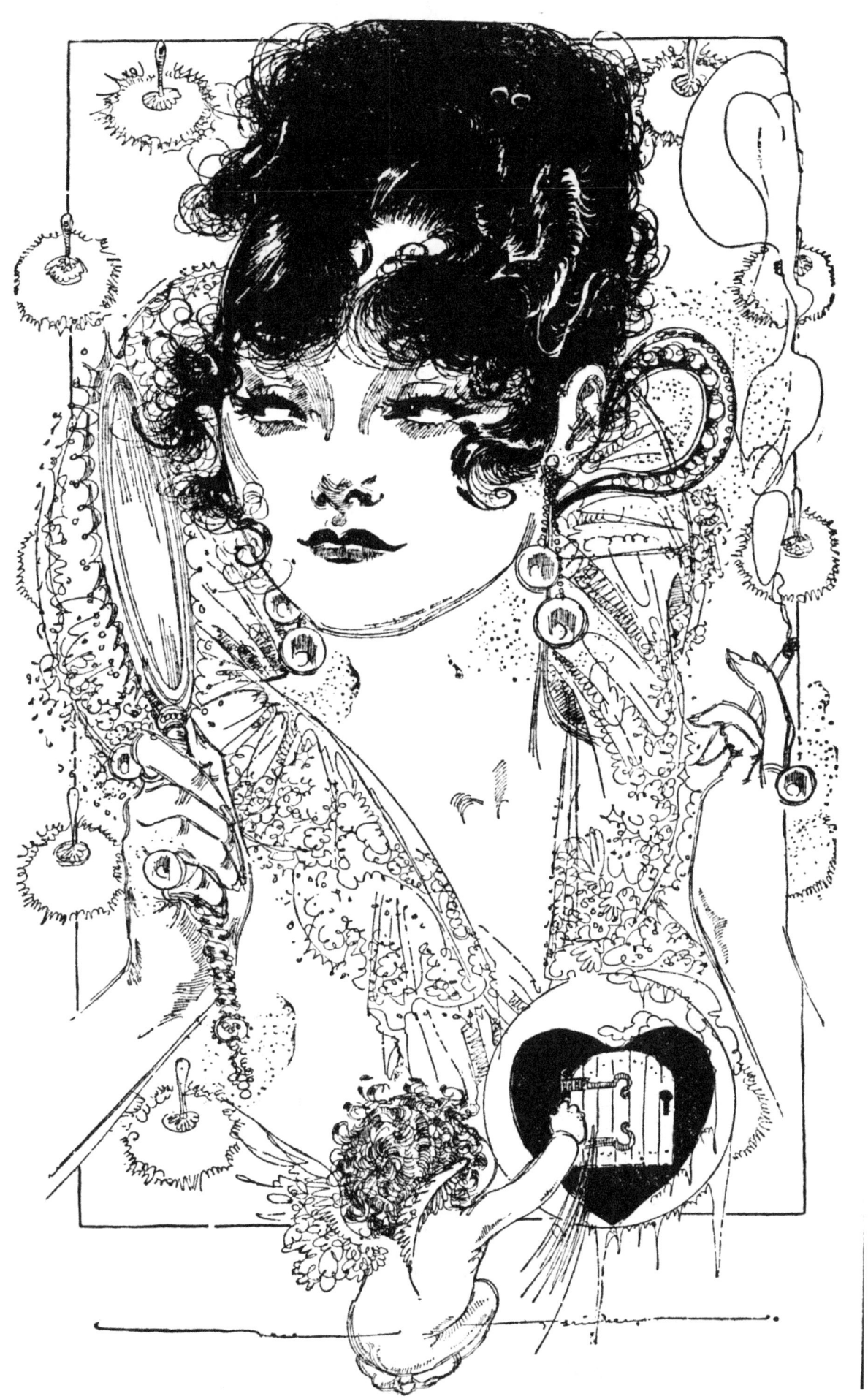

ABOUT THE ILLUSTRATION ON THE REVERSE

Original publication: El Paso Herald (Texas)

Publication date: December 11, 1914

Title: "Nobody Home!"

Artist: Nell Brinkley

© Copyright 2015 by Synchronista LLC & ClickAmericana.com

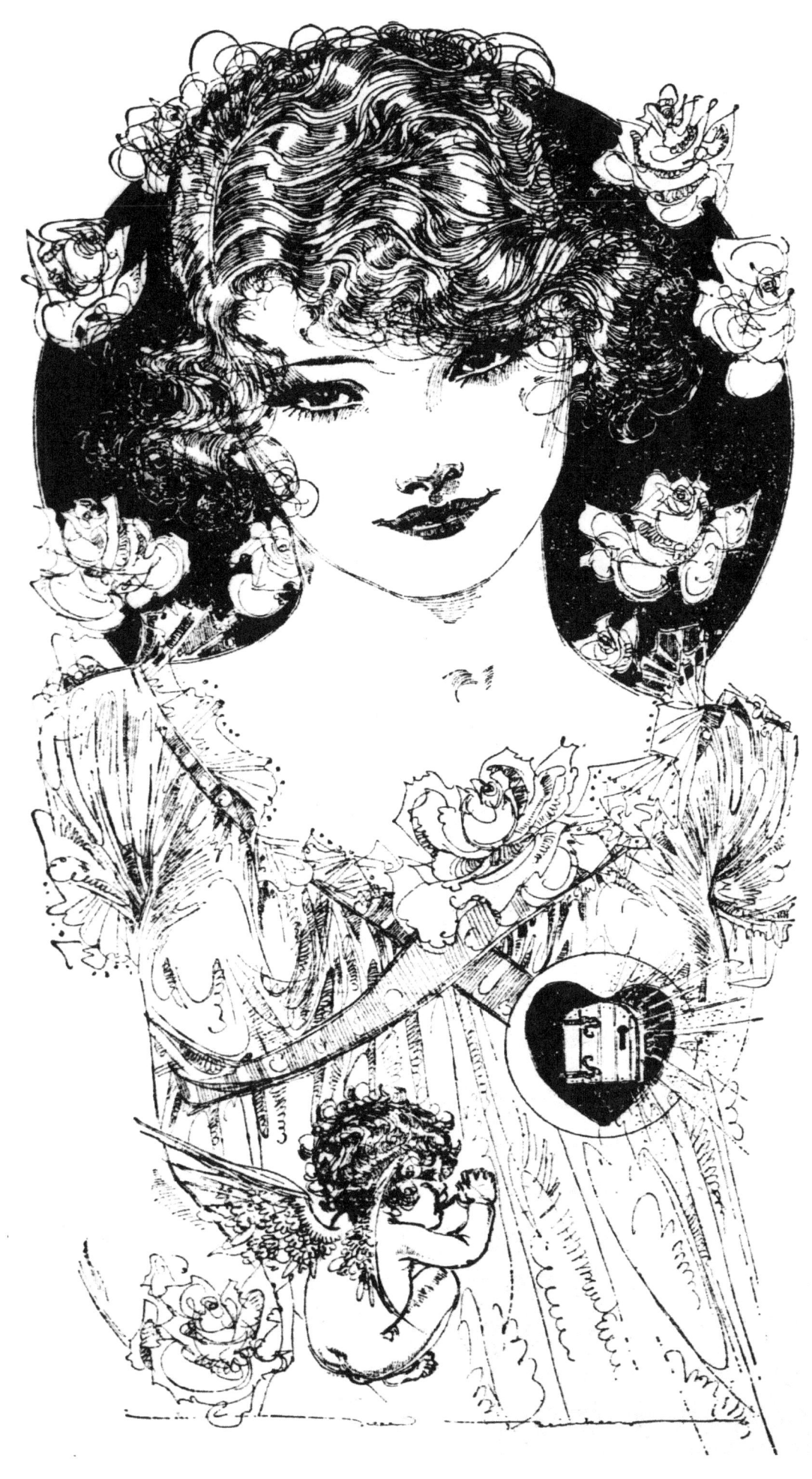

ABOUT THE ILLUSTRATION ON THE REVERSE

Original publication: The Topeka State Journal (Kansas)

Publication date: December 26, 1914

Title: "Somebody Home!"

Artist: Nell Brinkley

© Copyright 2015 by Synchronista LLC & ClickAmericana.com

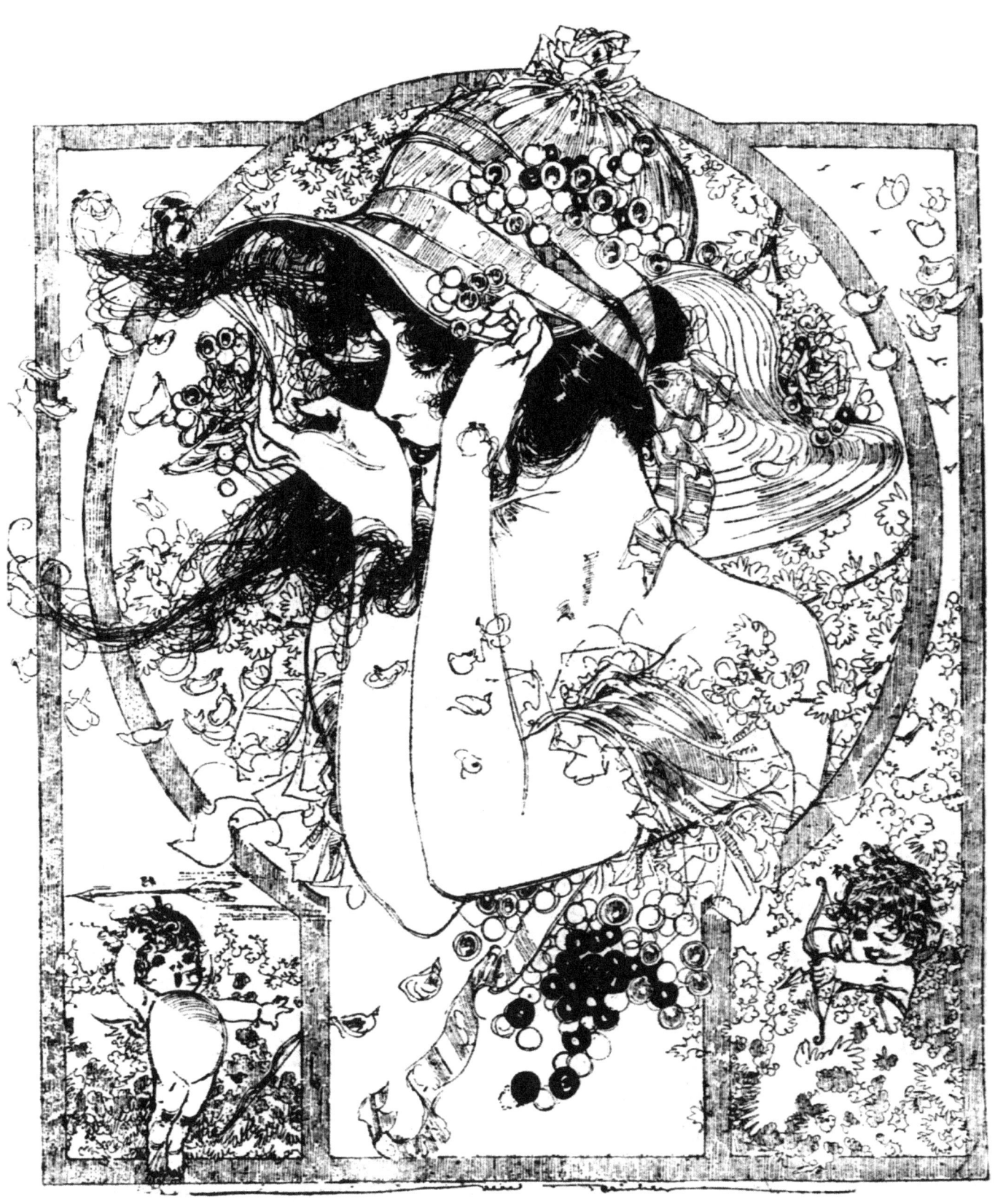

ABOUT THE ILLUSTRATION ON THE REVERSE

Original publication: El Paso Herald (Texas)

Publication date: May 23, 1916

Title: "Dear-Season Accident"

Artist: Nell Brinkley

© Copyright 2015 by Synchronista LLC & ClickAmericana.com

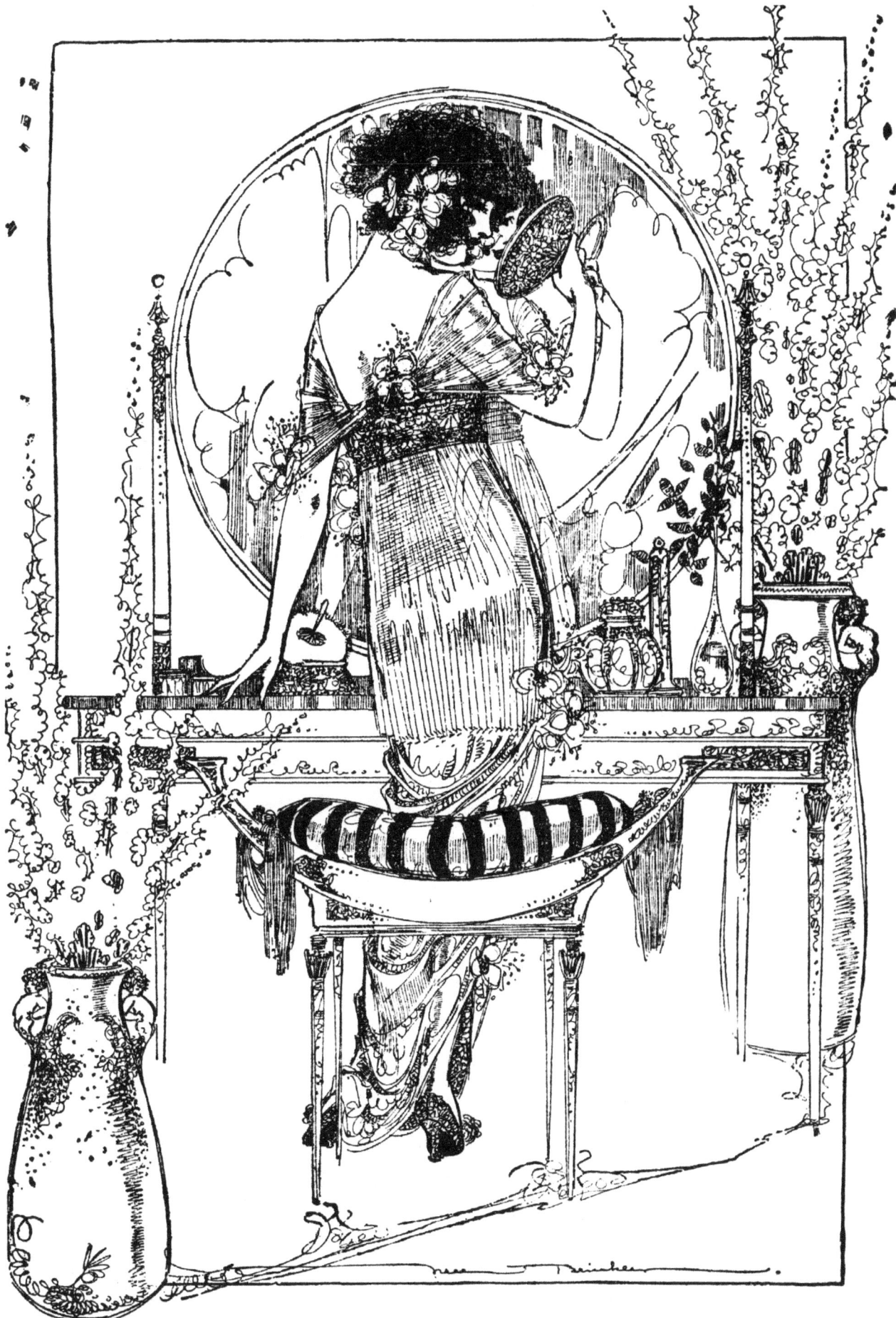

ABOUT THE ILLUSTRATION ON THE REVERSE

Original publication: The Topeka State Journal (Kansas)

Publication date: August 19, 1913

Title: "Flowers Instead of Jewels"

Artist: Nell Brinkley

© Copyright 2015 by Synchronista LLC & ClickAmericana.com

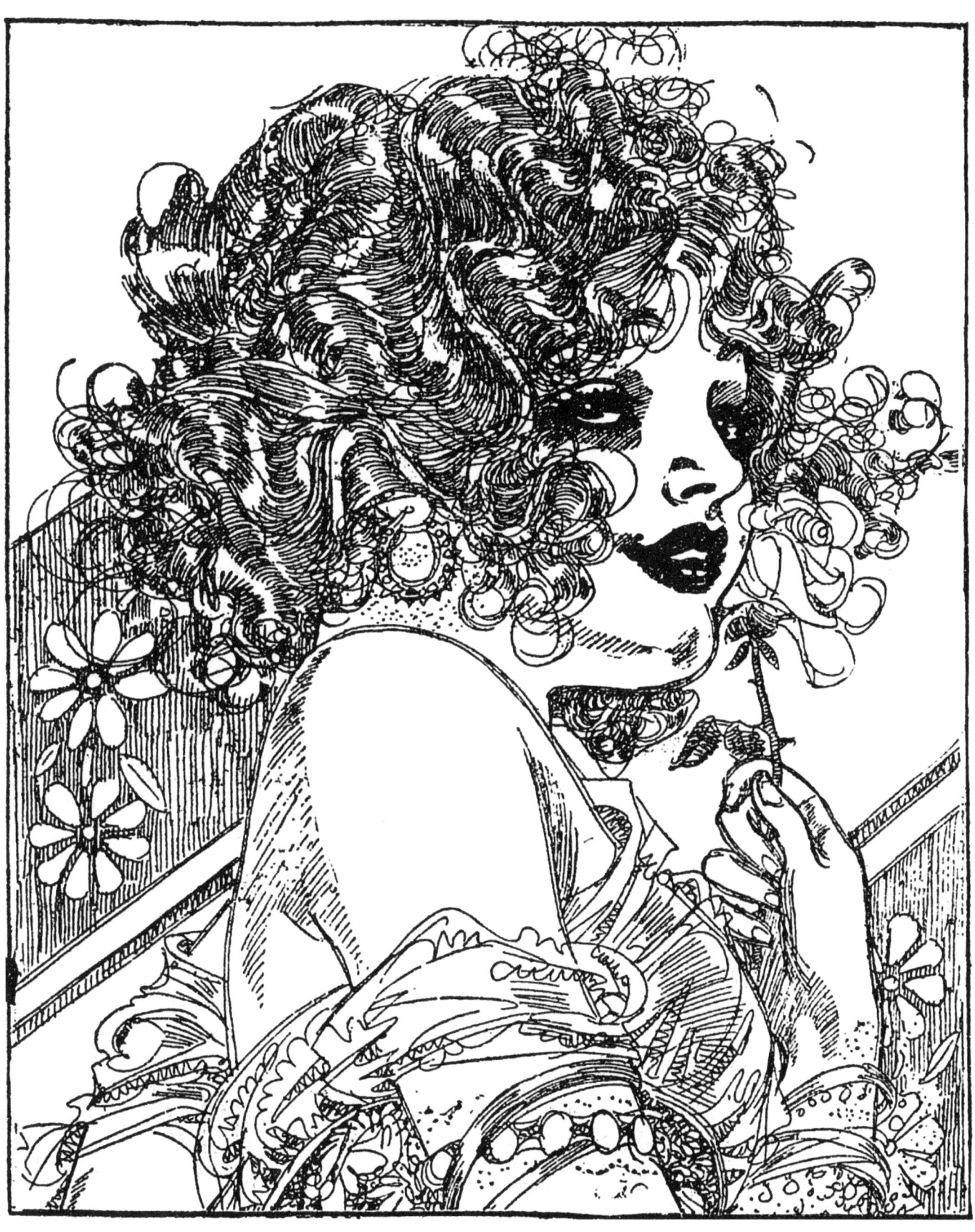

ABOUT THE ILLUSTRATION ON THE REVERSE

Original publication: The Times-Dispatch (Richmond, VA)

Publication date: March 16, 1913

Title: "The Two Dreamers"

Artist: Nell Brinkley

© Copyright 2015 by Synchronista LLC & ClickAmericana.com

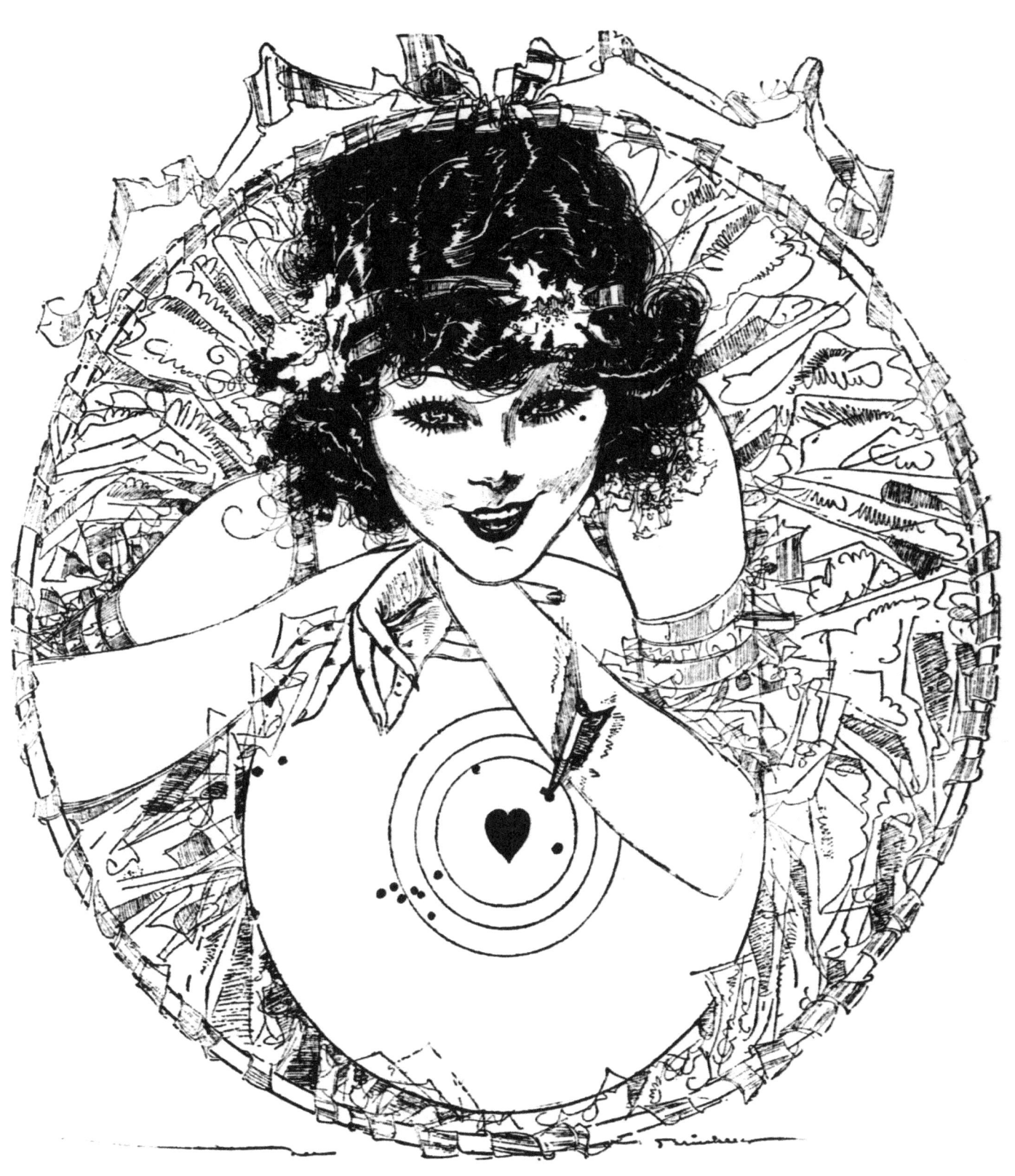

ABOUT THE ILLUSTRATION ON THE REVERSE

Original publication: El Paso Herald (Texas)

Publication date: March 10, 1917

Title: "Never Touched Me!"

Artist: Nell Brinkley

© Copyright 2015 by Synchronista LLC & ClickAmericana.com

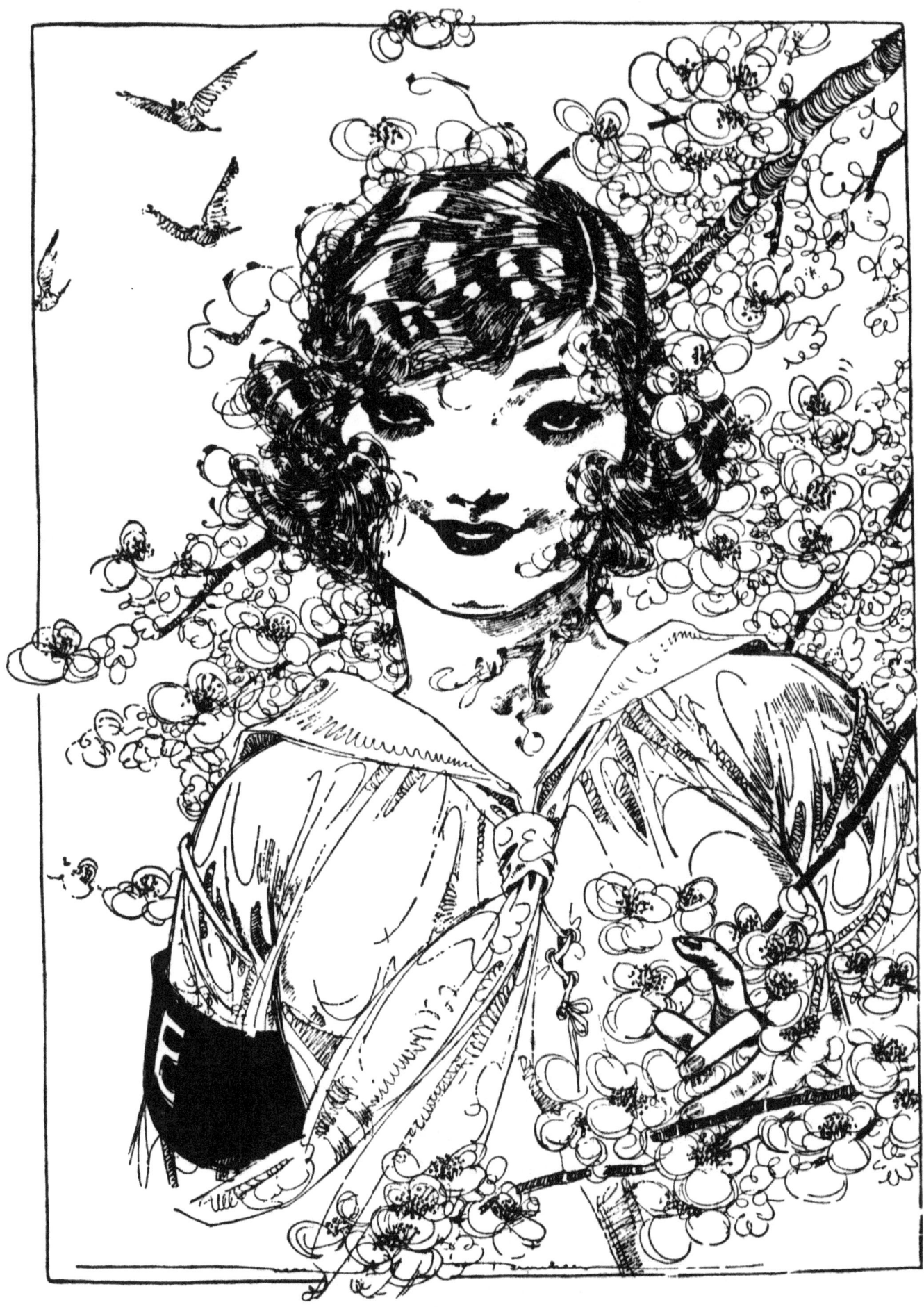

ABOUT THE ILLUSTRATION ON THE REVERSE

Original publication: Omaha Daily Bee (Nebraska)

Publication date: June 14, 1913

Title: "The Golden Age"

Artist: Nell Brinkley

© Copyright 2015 by Synchronista LLC & ClickAmericana.com

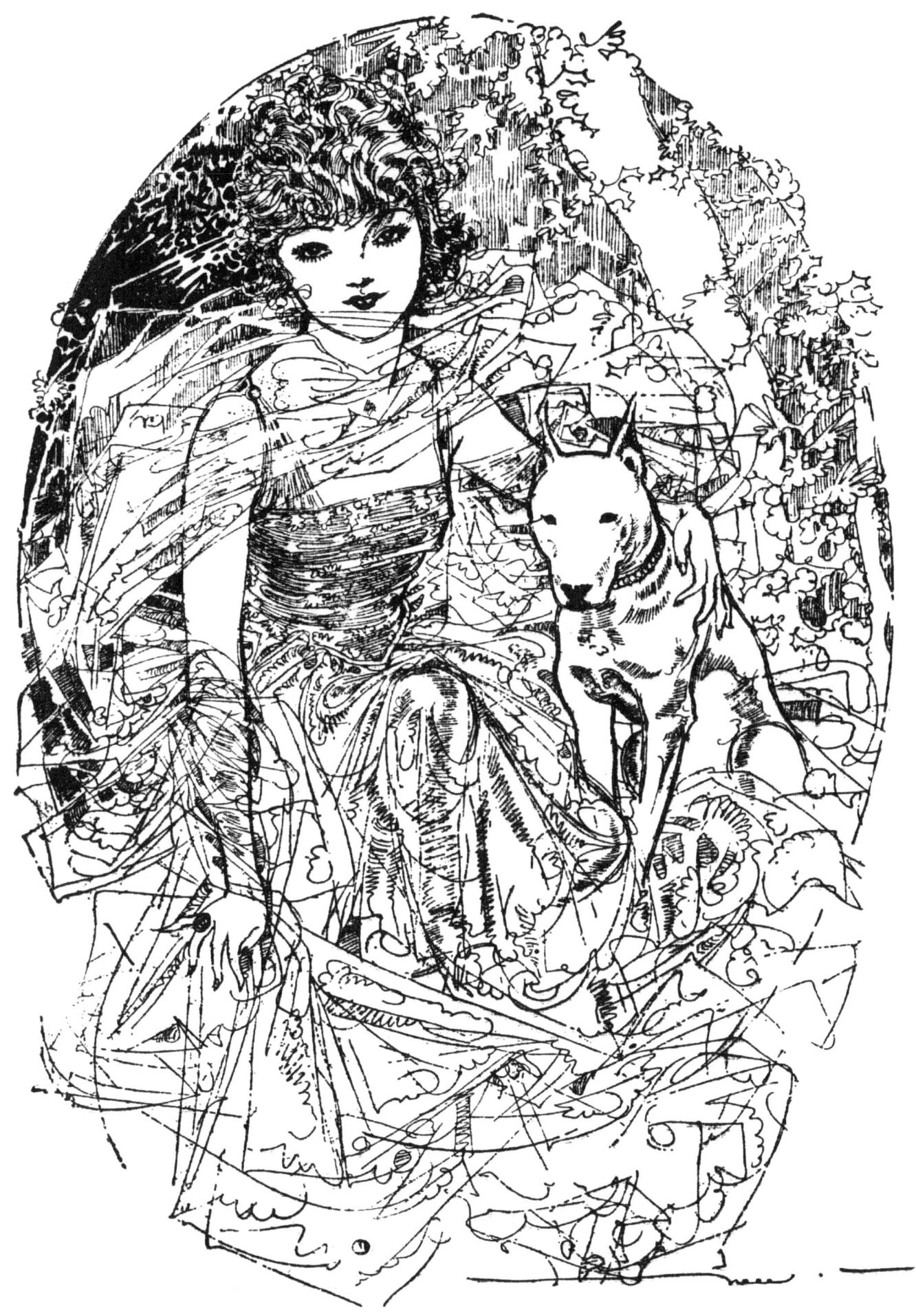

ABOUT THE ILLUSTRATION ON THE REVERSE

Original publication: The Topeka State Journal (Kansas)

Publication date: June 17, 1916

Title: "A Dangerous Fashion"

Artist: Nell Brinkley

© Copyright 2015 by Synchronista LLC & ClickAmericana.com

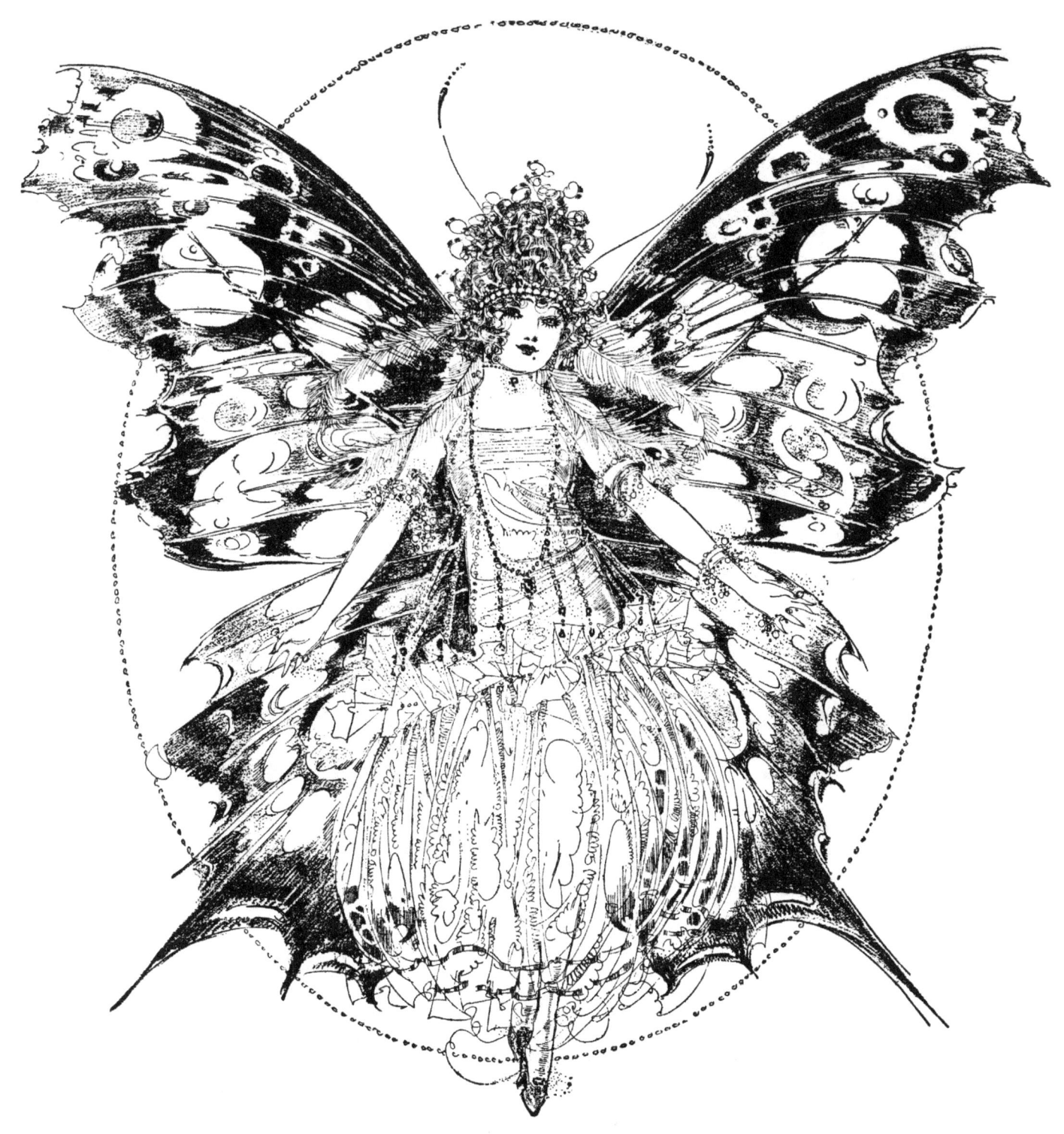

ABOUT THE ILLUSTRATION ON THE REVERSE

Original publication: The Topeka State Journal (Kansas)

Publication date: October 02, 1915

Title: "The Last of Summer"

Artist: Nell Brinkley

© Copyright 2015 by Synchronista LLC & ClickAmericana.com

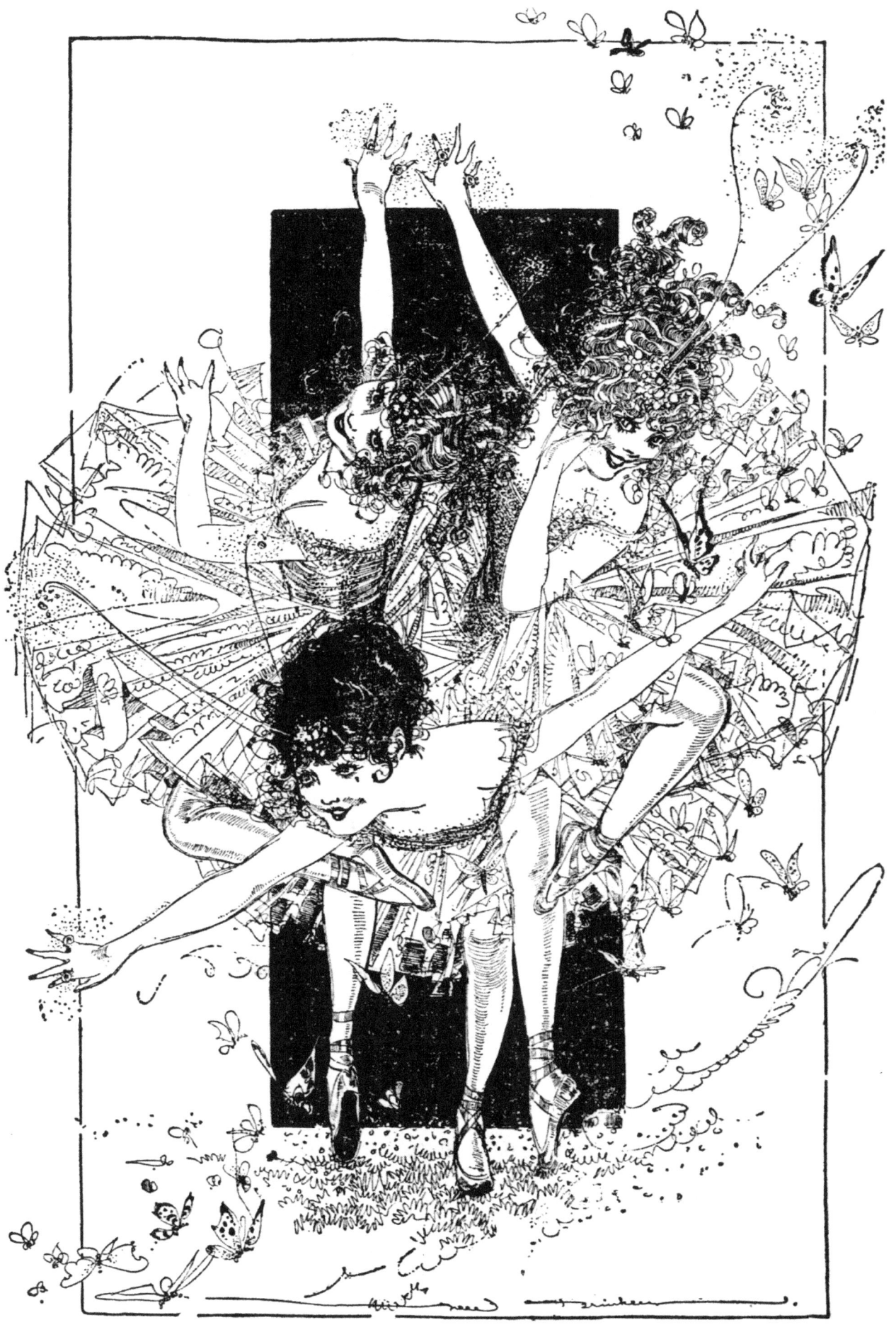

ABOUT THE ILLUSTRATION ON THE REVERSE

Original publication: El Paso Herald (Texas)

Publication date: October 14, 1914

Title: "Birds of a Feather - Butterflies"

Artist: Nell Brinkley

© Copyright 2015 by Synchronista LLC & ClickAmericana.com

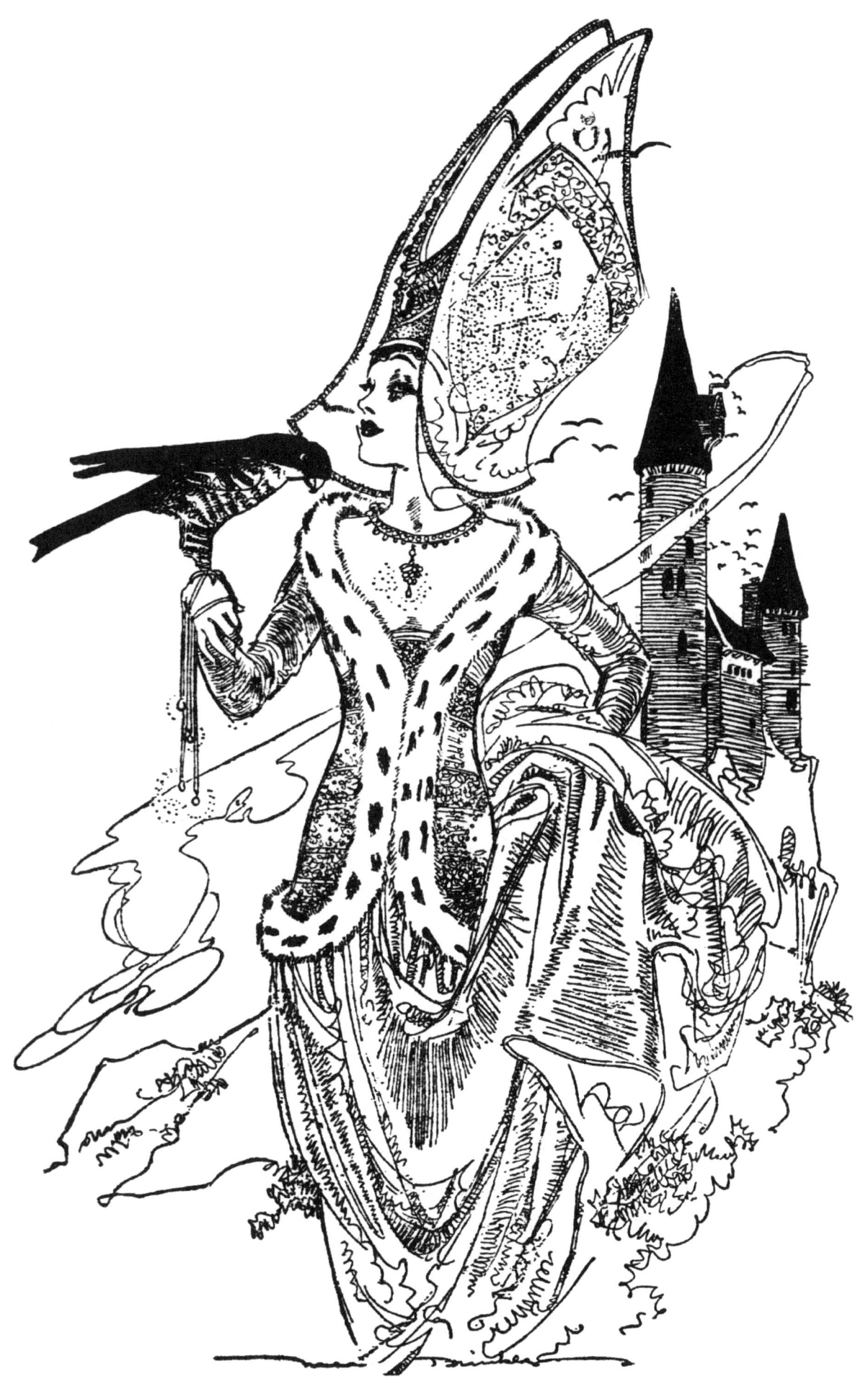

ABOUT THE ILLUSTRATION ON THE REVERSE

Original publication: El Paso Herald (Texas)

Publication date: September 11, 1912

Title: "The First Outdoor Girl"

Artist: Nell Brinkley

© Copyright 2015 by Synchronista LLC & ClickAmericana.com

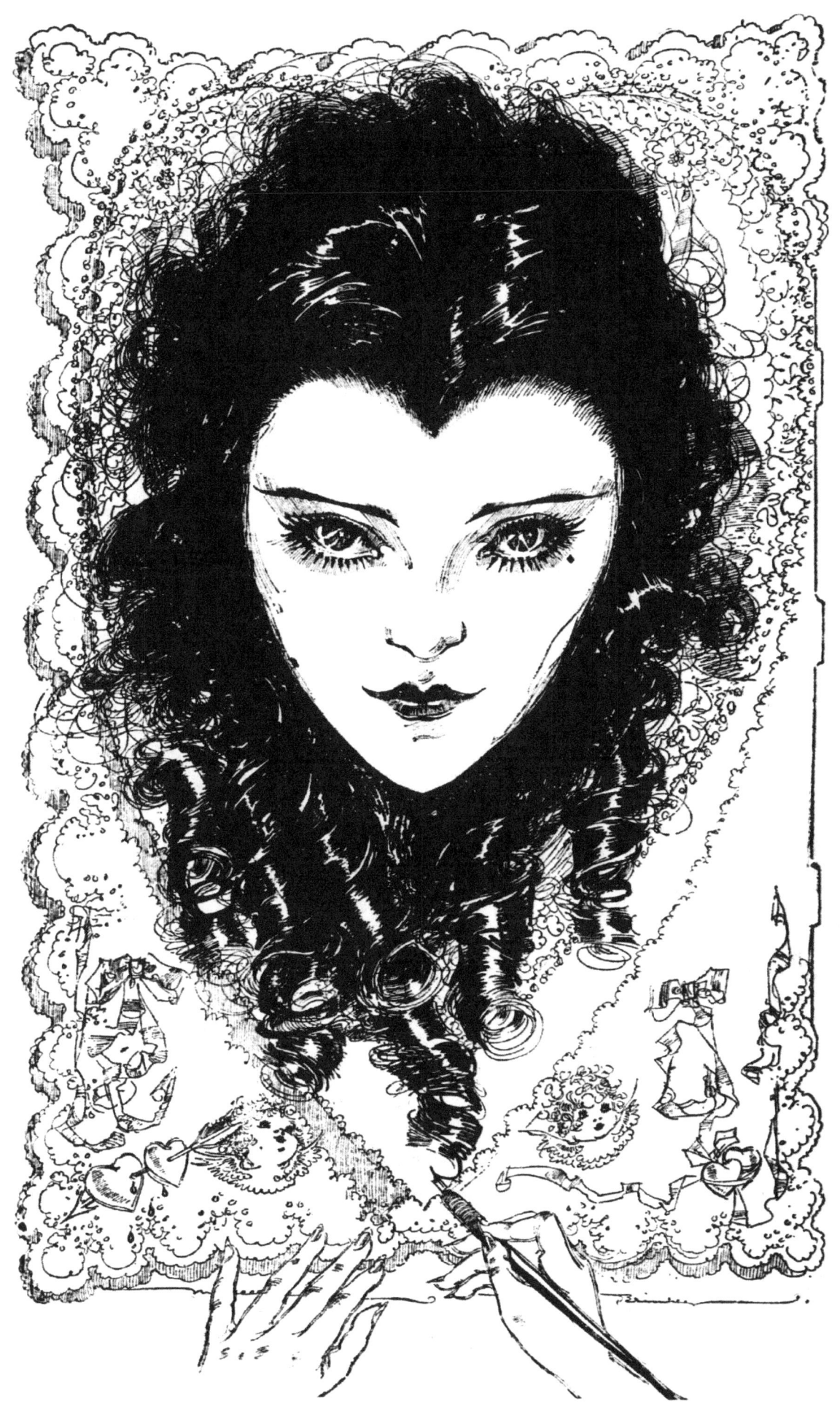

ABOUT THE ILLUSTRATION ON THE REVERSE

Original publication:	El Paso Herald (Texas)
Publication date:	February 14, 1917
Title:	"My Valentine"
Artist:	Nell Brinkley

© Copyright 2015 by Synchronista LLC & ClickAmericana.com

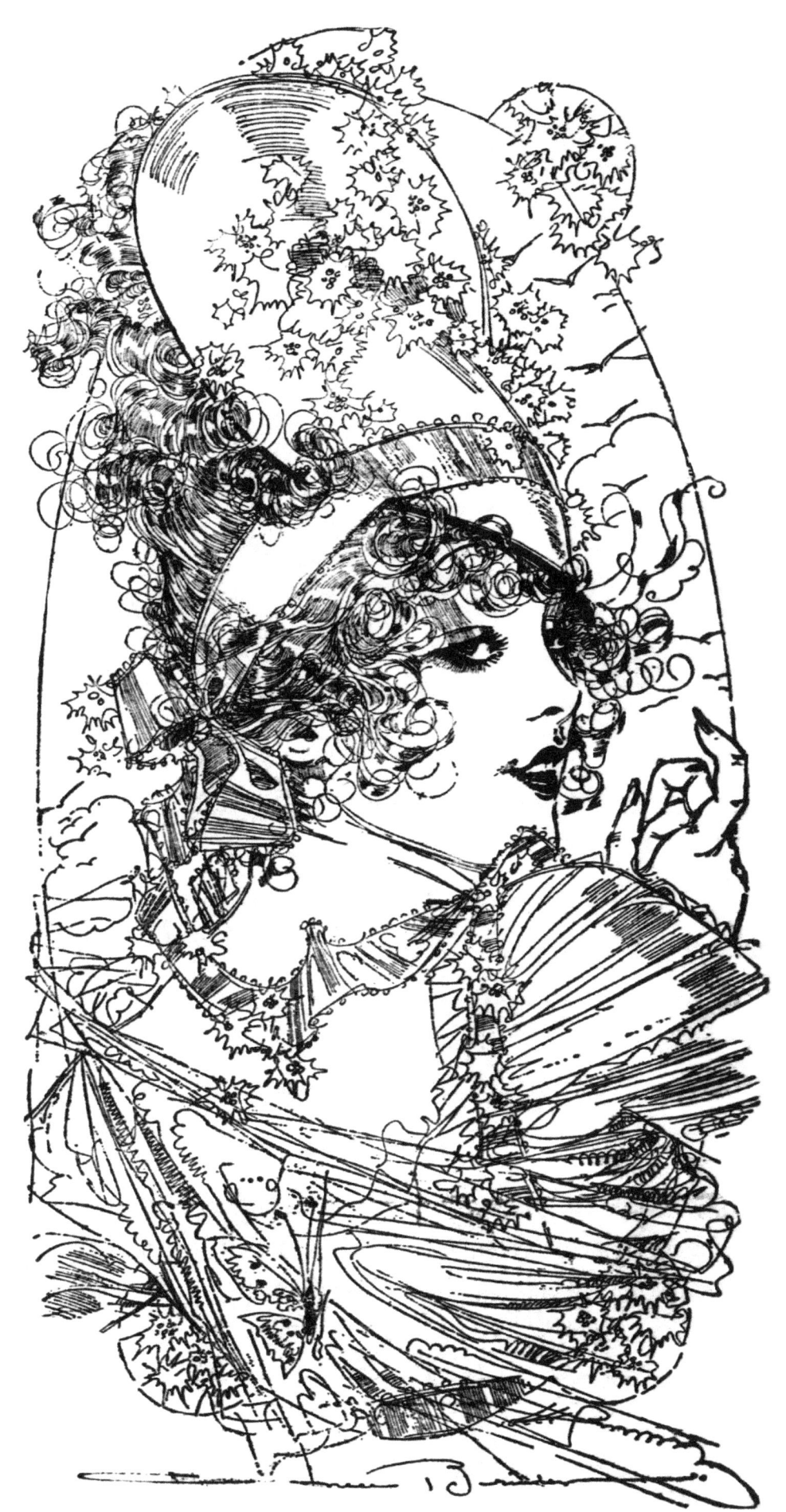

ABOUT THE ILLUSTRATION ON THE REVERSE

Original publication: El Paso Herald (Texas)

Publication date: June 23, 1917

Title: "A Born Flirt"

Artist: Nell Brinkley

© Copyright 2015 by Synchronista LLC & ClickAmericana.com

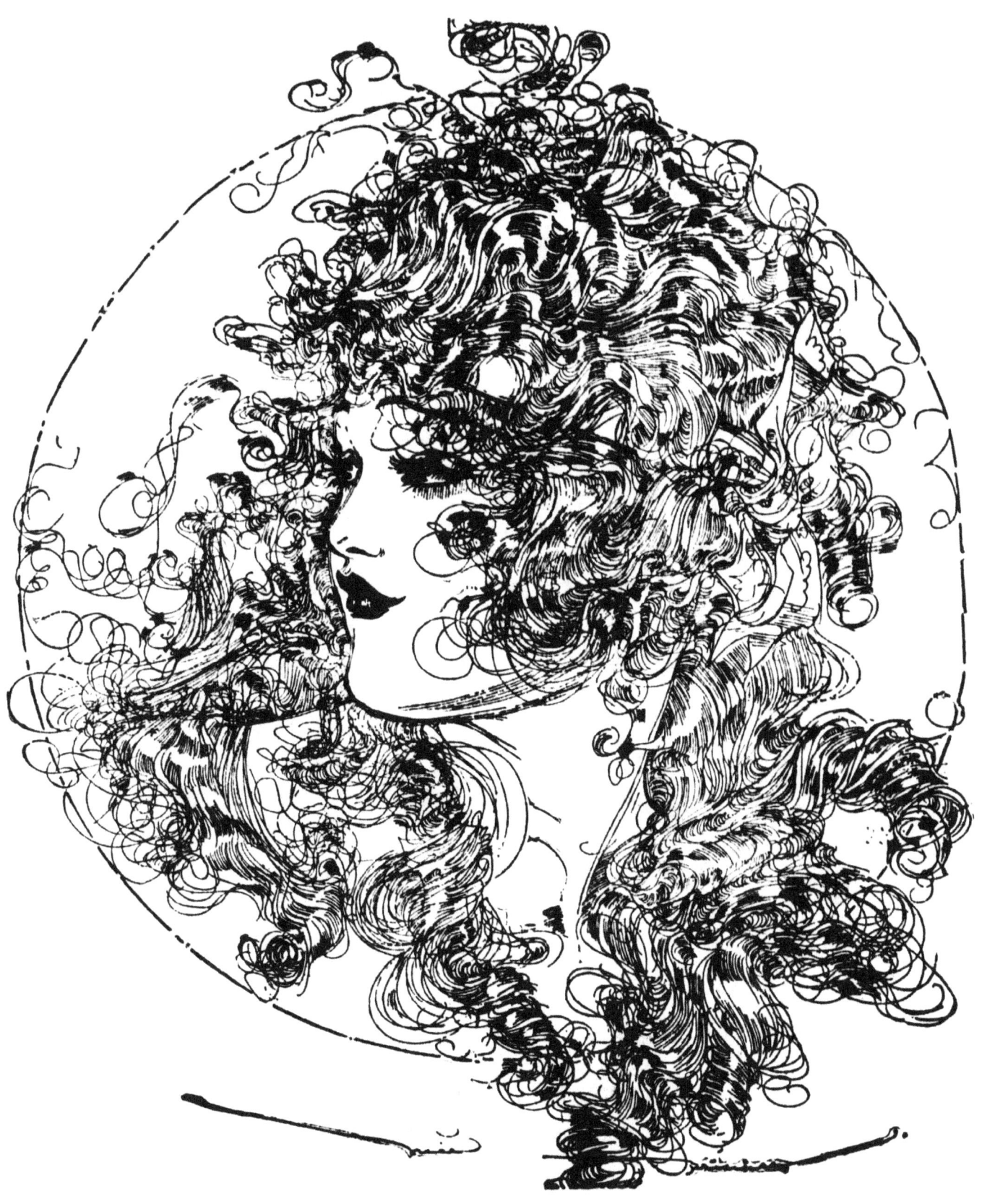

ABOUT THE ILLUSTRATION ON THE REVERSE

Original publication: Omaha Daily Bee (Nebraska)

Publication date: February 24, 1916

Title: "Her Likeness"

Artist: Nell Brinkley

© Copyright 2015 by Synchronista LLC & ClickAmericana.com

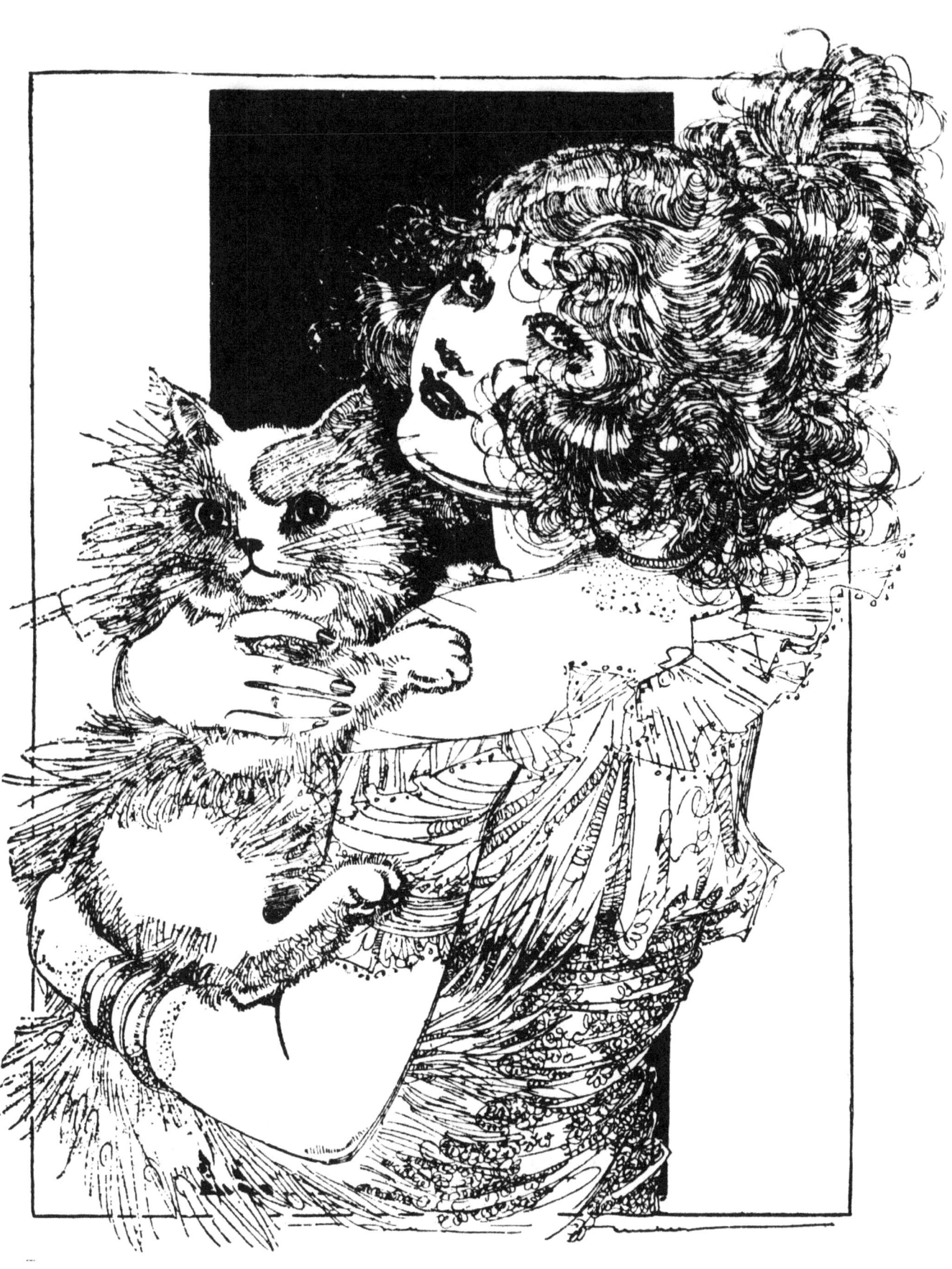

ABOUT THE ILLUSTRATION ON THE REVERSE

Original publication: Omaha Daily Bee (Nebraska)

Publication date: December 23, 1913

Title: "Two Cats"

Artist: Nell Brinkley

© Copyright 2015 by Synchronista LLC & ClickAmericana.com

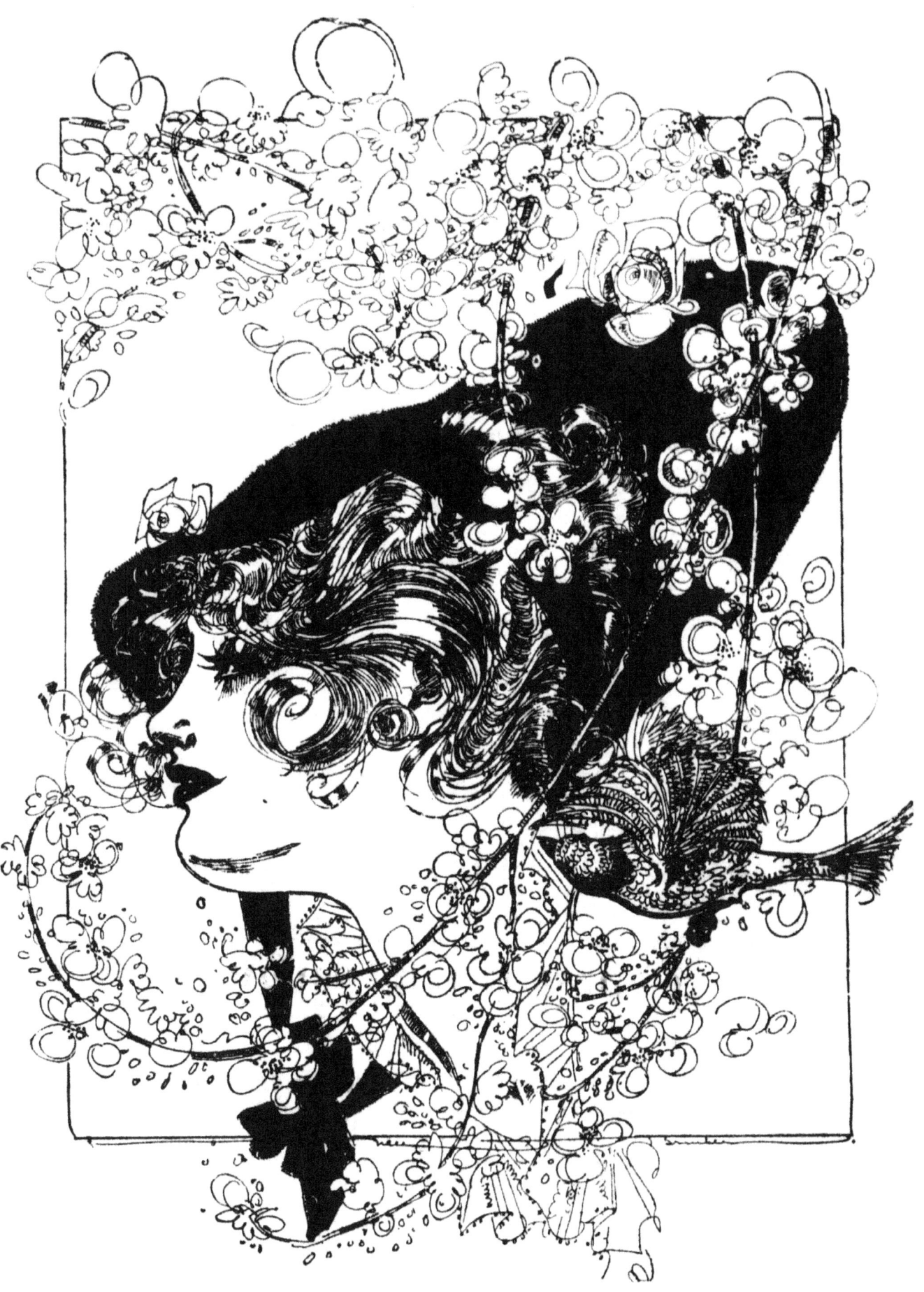

ABOUT THE ILLUSTRATION ON THE REVERSE

Original publication: Omaha Daily Bee (Nebraska)

Publication date: May 02, 1914

Title: "Peach Blossoms"

Artist: Nell Brinkley

© Copyright 2015 by Synchronista LLC & ClickAmericana.com

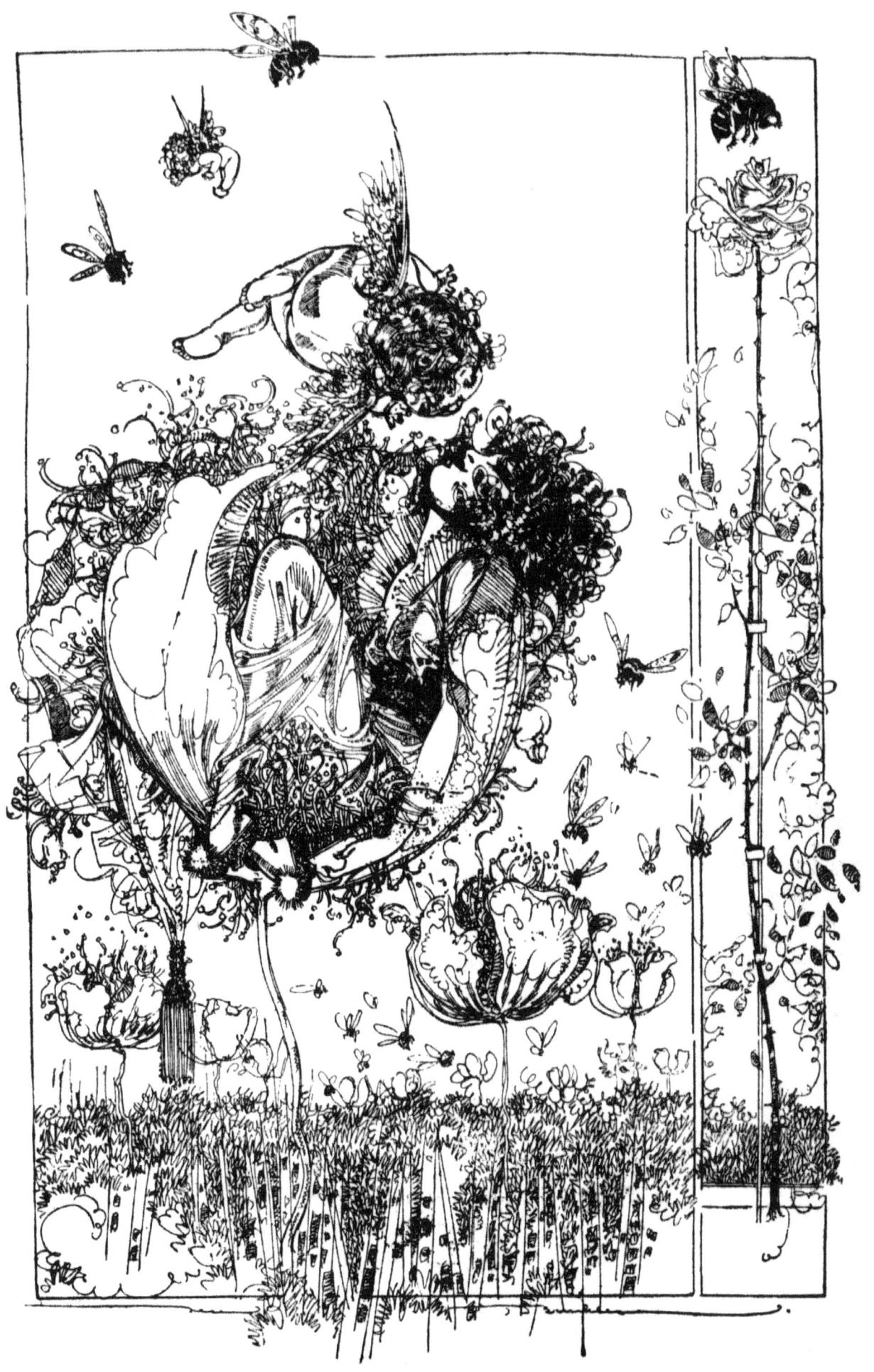

ABOUT THE ILLUSTRATION ON THE REVERSE

Original publication: Omaha Daily Bee (Nebraska)

Publication date: February 19, 1914

Title: "The Bee and the Flower"

Artist: Nell Brinkley

© Copyright 2015 by Synchronista LLC & ClickAmericana.com

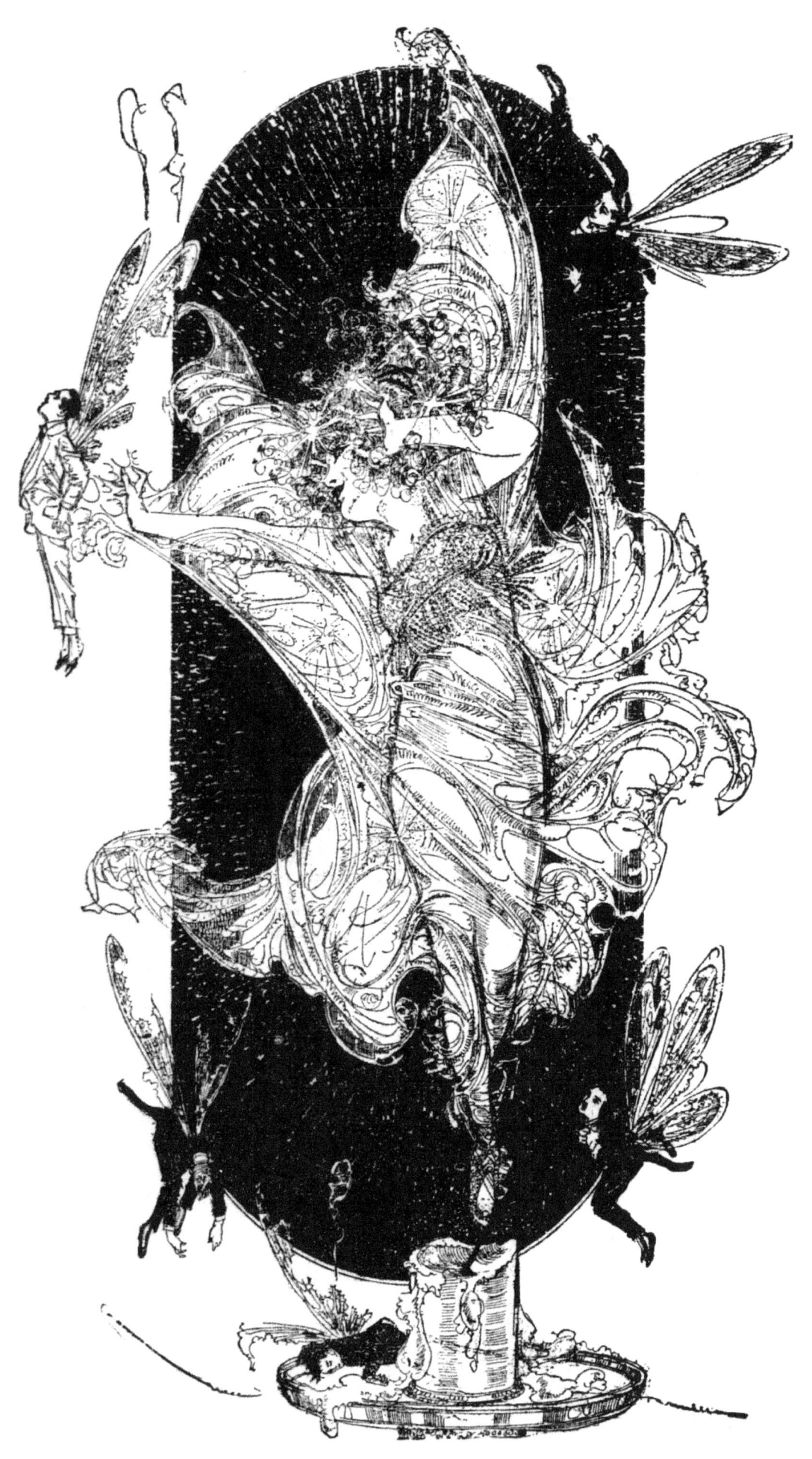

ABOUT THE ILLUSTRATION ON THE REVERSE

Original publication: El Paso Herald (Texas)

Publication date: December 30, 1914

Title: "Moths and the Flame"

Artist: Nell Brinkley

© Copyright 2015 by Synchronista LLC & ClickAmericana.com

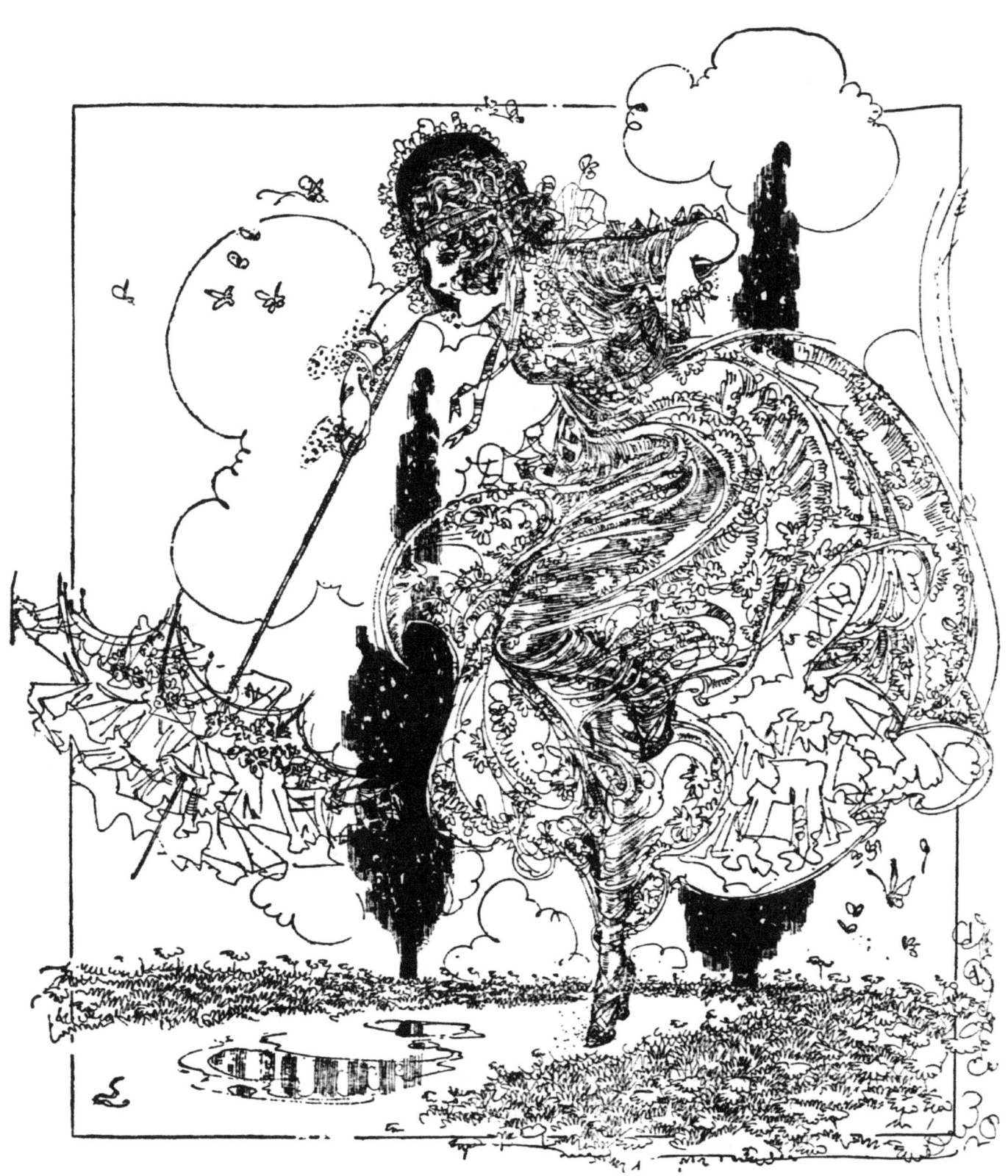

ABOUT THE ILLUSTRATION ON THE REVERSE

Original publication: El Paso Herald (Texas)

Publication date: June 26, 1915

Title: "Oh, Eve, Thy Name is Mystery"

Artist: Nell Brinkley

© Copyright 2015 by Synchronista LLC & ClickAmericana.com

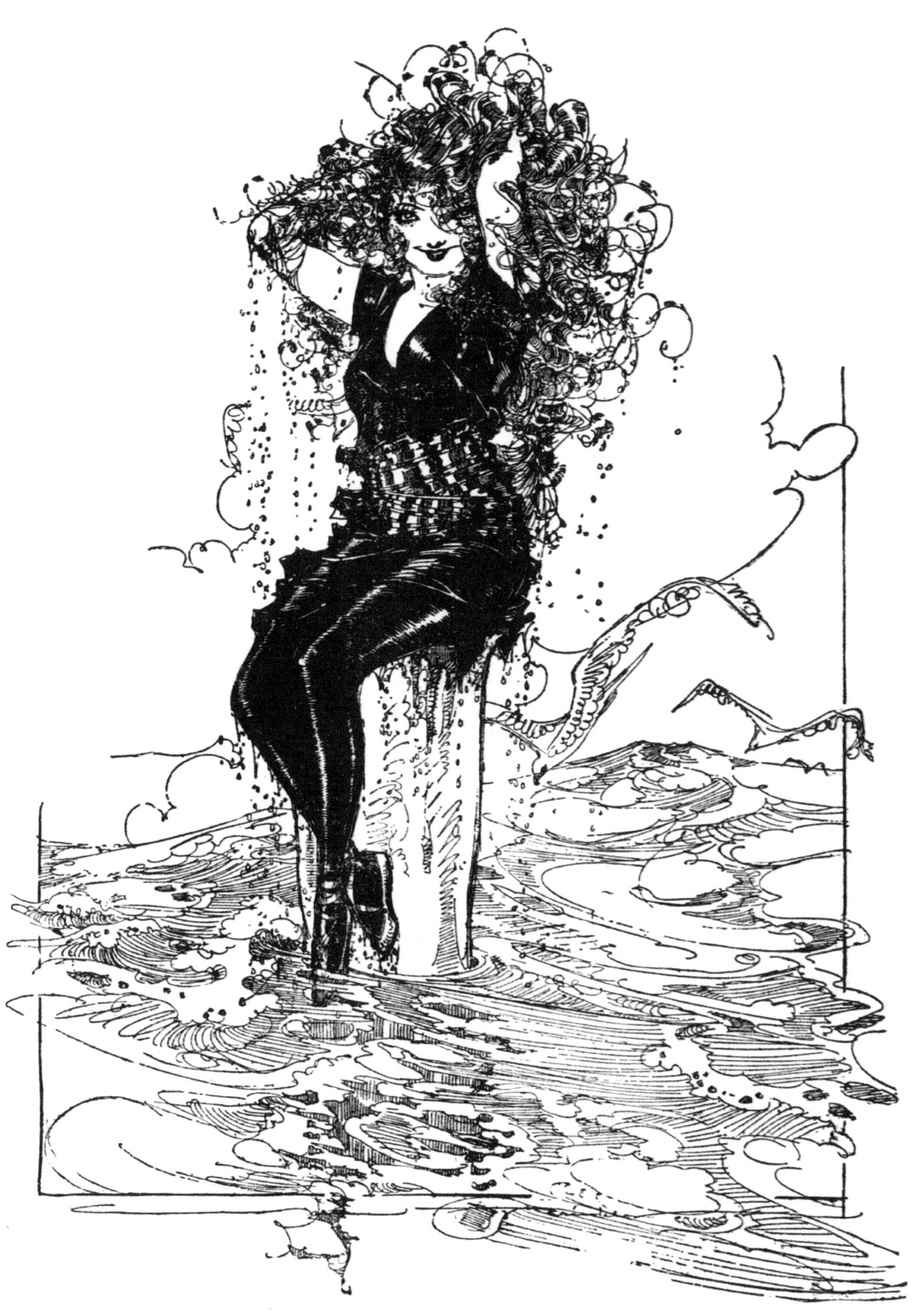

ABOUT THE ILLUSTRATION ON THE REVERSE

Original publication: El Paso Herald (Texas)

Publication date: June 27, 1914

Title: "A Peril of the Sea"

Artist: Nell Brinkley

© Copyright 2015 by Synchronista LLC & ClickAmericana.com

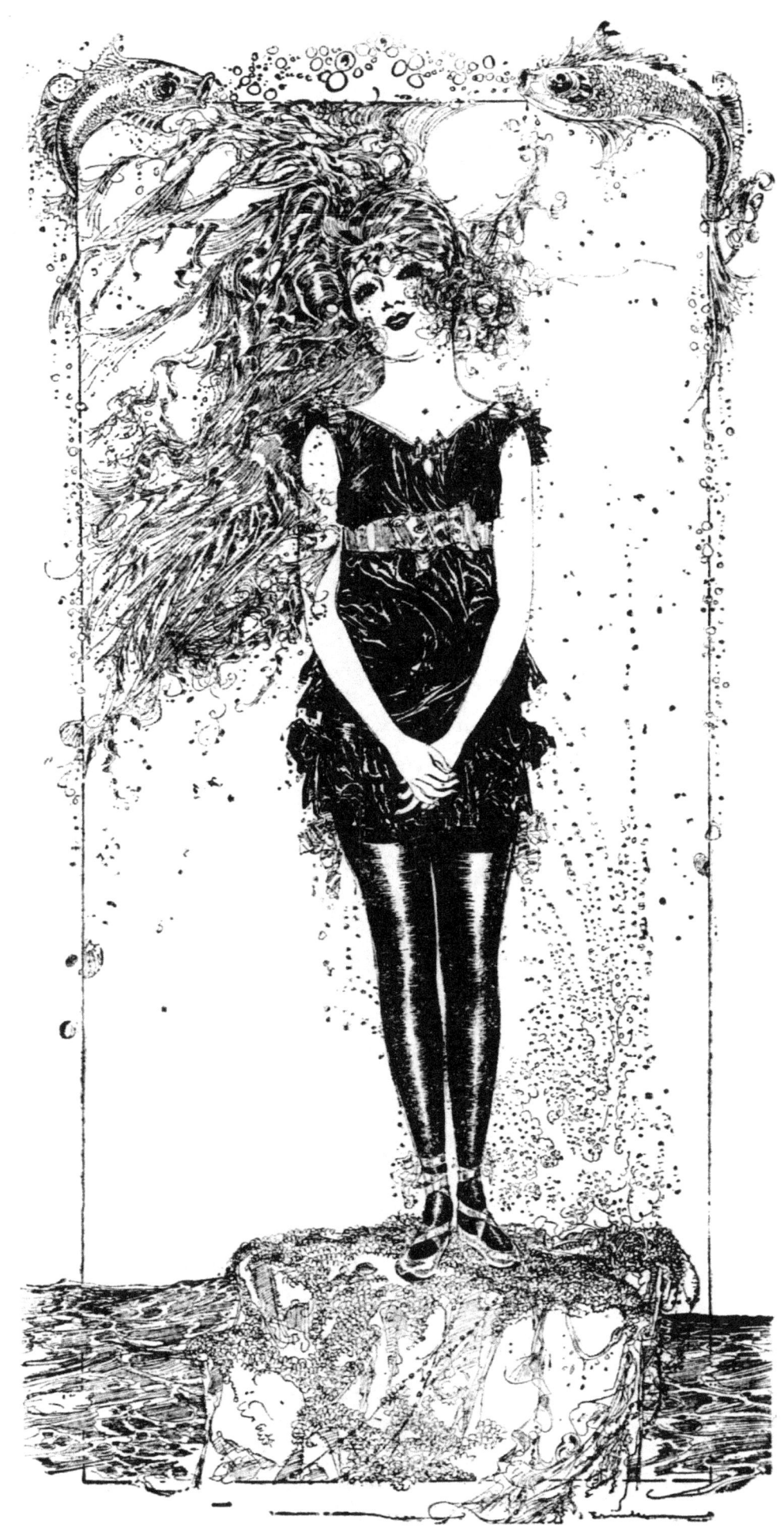

ABOUT THE ILLUSTRATION ON THE REVERSE

Original publication: El Paso Herald (Texas)

Publication date: May 9, 1917

Title: "One Swallow"

Artist: Nell Brinkley

© Copyright 2015 by Synchronista LLC & ClickAmericana.com

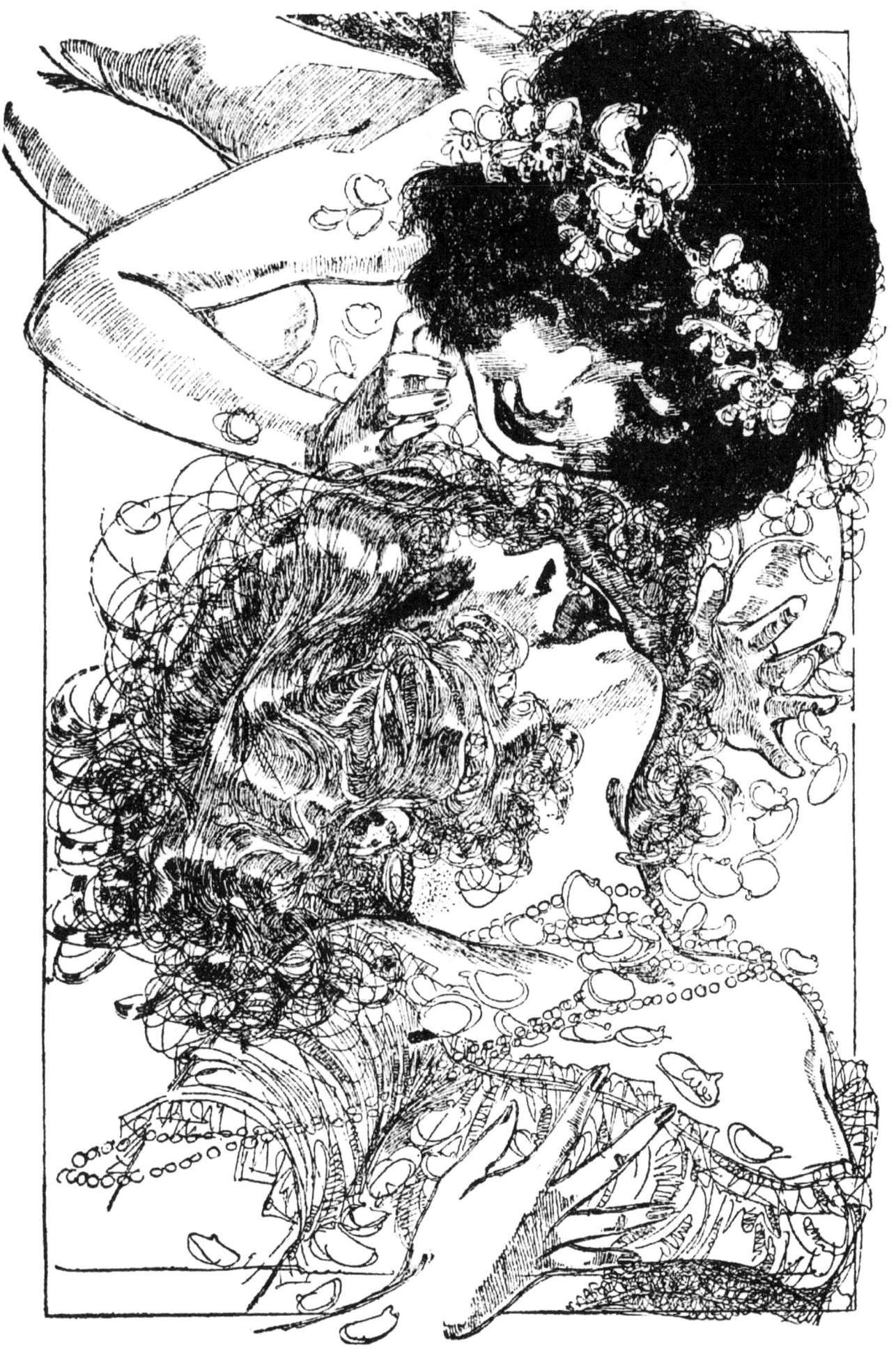

ABOUT THE ILLUSTRATION ON THE REVERSE

Original publication: The Salt Lake Tribune (Utah)

Publication date: October 27, 1912

Title: "Beauty and Youth"

Artist: Nell Brinkley

© Copyright 2015 by Synchronista LLC & ClickAmericana.com

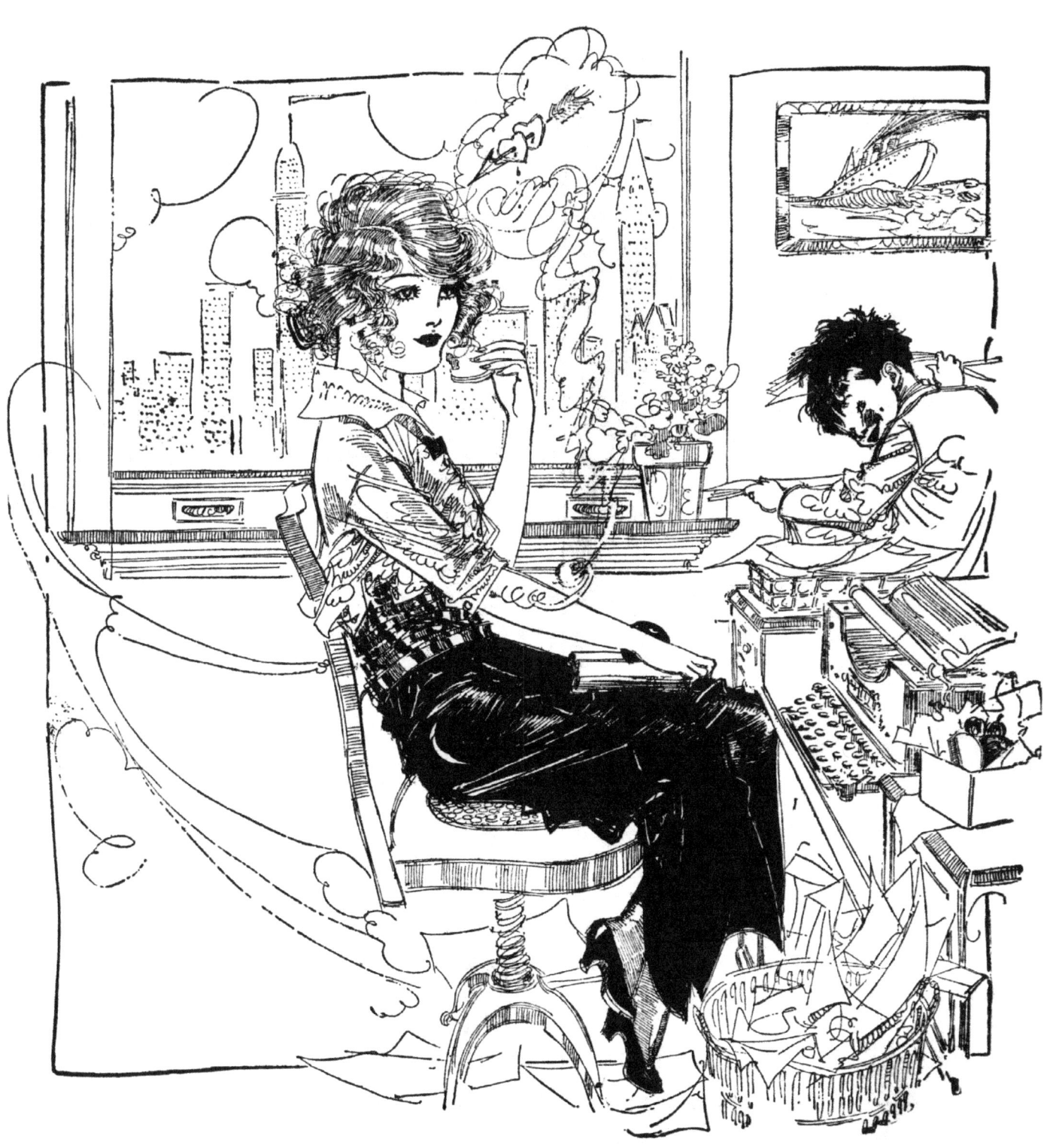

ABOUT THE ILLUSTRATION ON THE REVERSE

Original publication: El Paso Herald (Texas)

Publication date: November 07, 1914

Title: "Worship and Treachery"

Artist: Nell Brinkley

© Copyright 2015 by Synchronista LLC & ClickAmericana.com

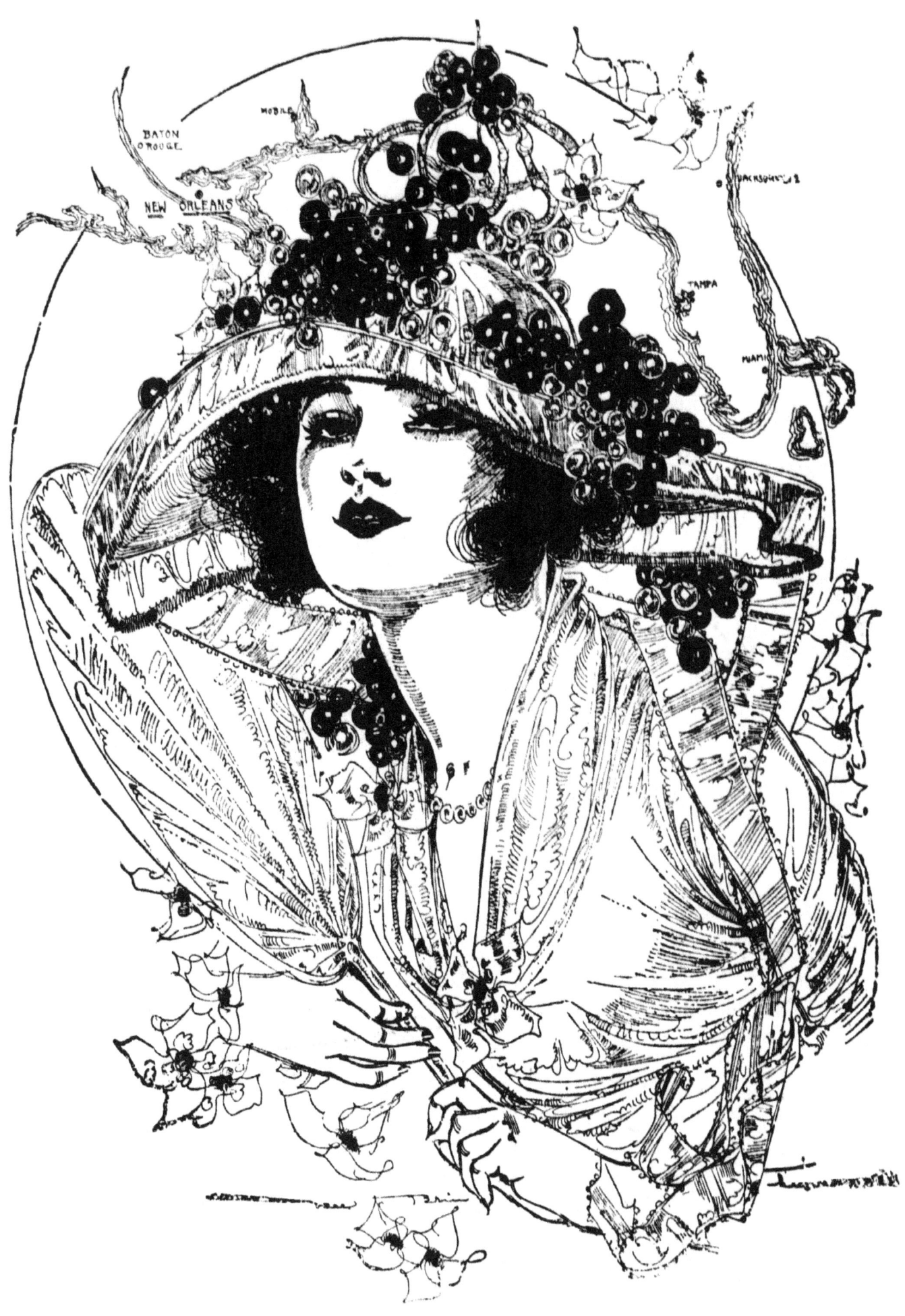

ABOUT THE ILLUSTRATION ON THE REVERSE

Original publication: Omaha Daily Bee (Nebraska)

Publication date: October 27, 1915

Title: "I Know a Girl There!" (New Orleans)

Artist: Nell Brinkley

© Copyright 2015 by Synchronista LLC & ClickAmericana.com

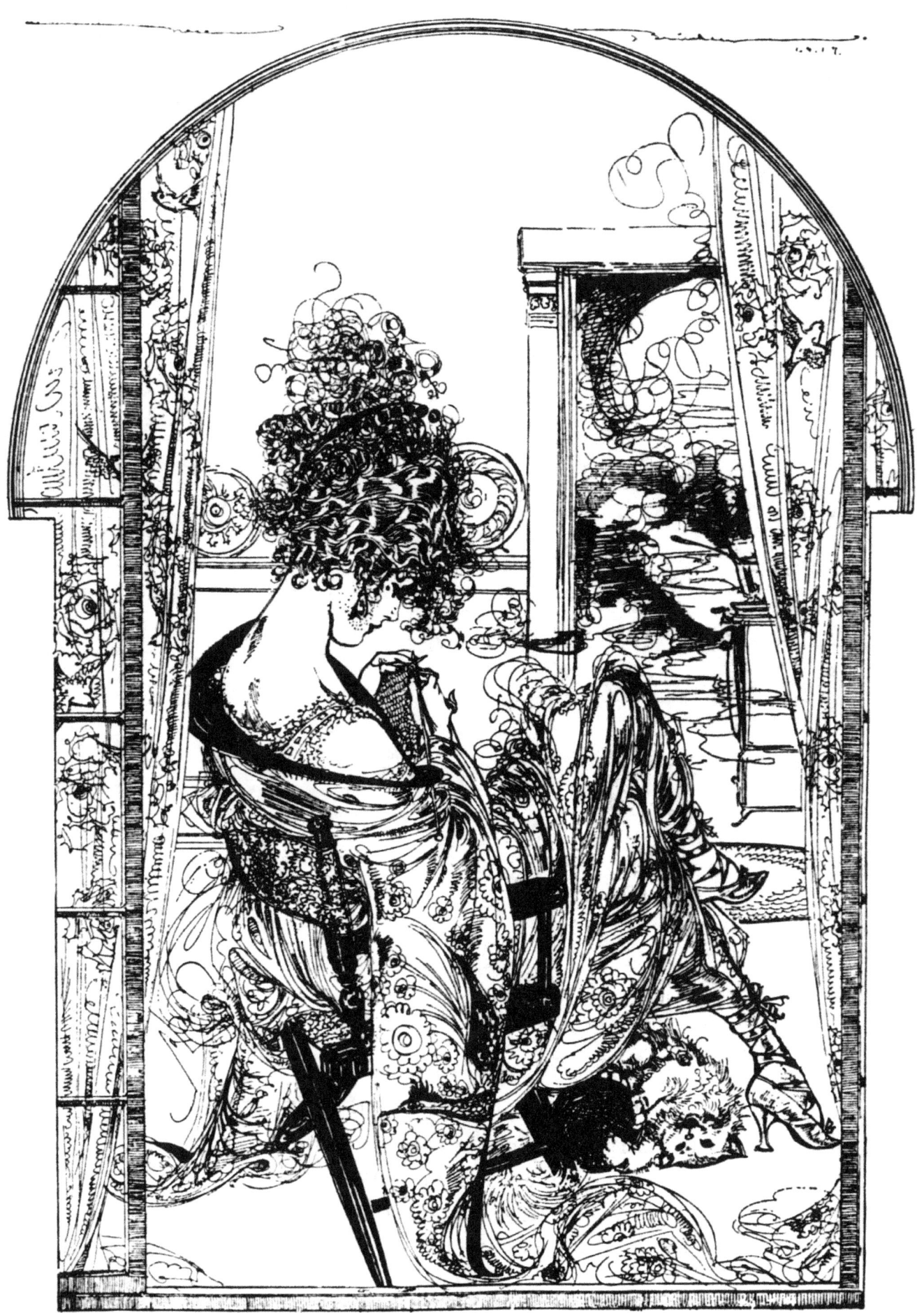

ABOUT THE ILLUSTRATION ON THE REVERSE

Original publication: The Washington Times (DC)

Publication date: November 15, 1917

Title: "Sister Susie"

Artist: Nell Brinkley

© Copyright 2015 by Synchronista LLC & ClickAmericana.com

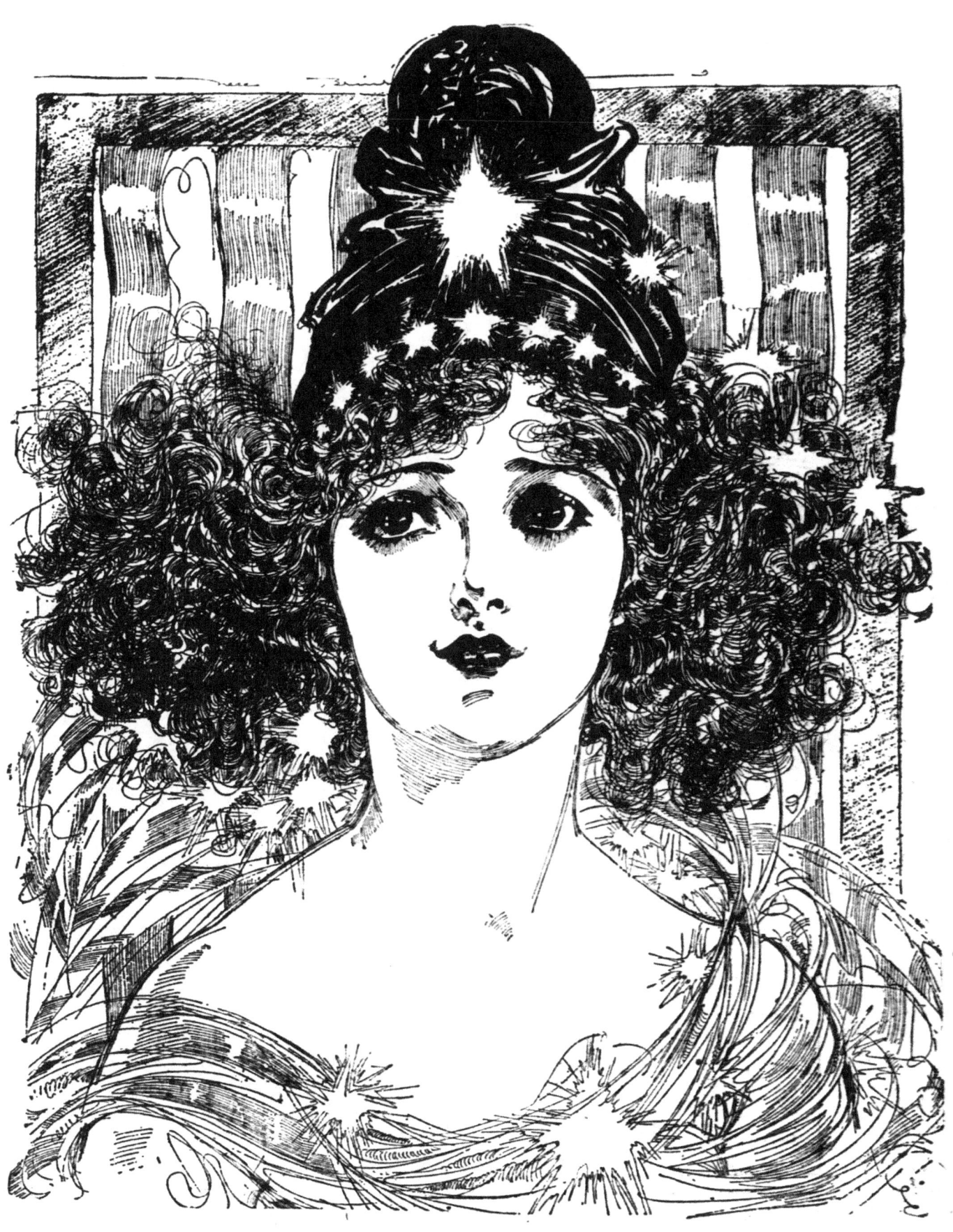

ABOUT THE ILLUSTRATION ON THE REVERSE

Original publication: El Paso Herald (Texas)

Publication date: July 06, 1918

Title: "The Face That Launched A Thousand Ships"

Artist: Nell Brinkley

© Copyright 2015 by Synchronista LLC & ClickAmericana.com

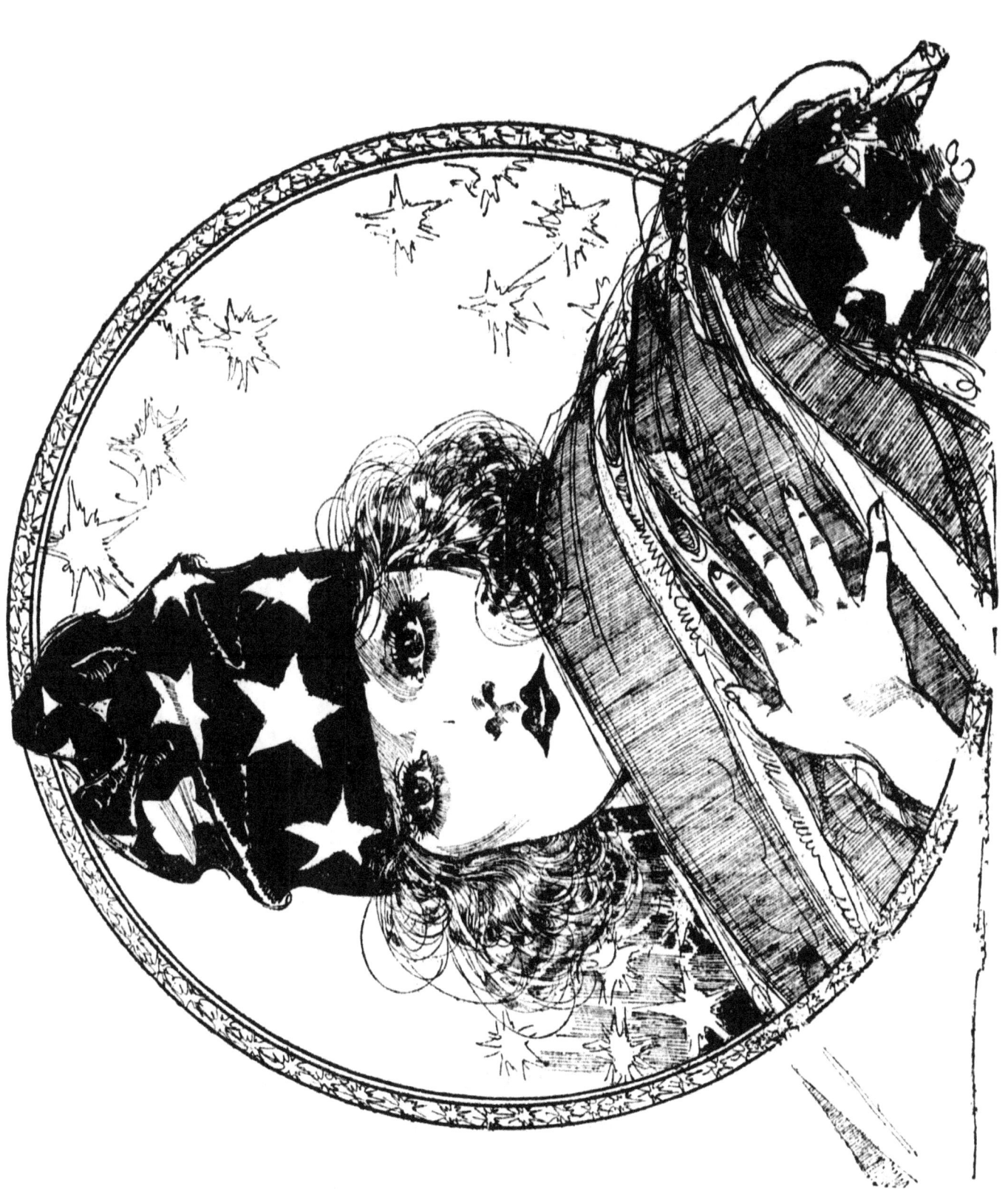

ABOUT THE ILLUSTRATION ON THE REVERSE

Original publication: El Paso Herald (Texas)

Publication date: April 14, 1917

Title: "The Most Beautiful Woman"

Artist: Nell Brinkley

© Copyright 2015 by Synchronista LLC & ClickAmericana.com

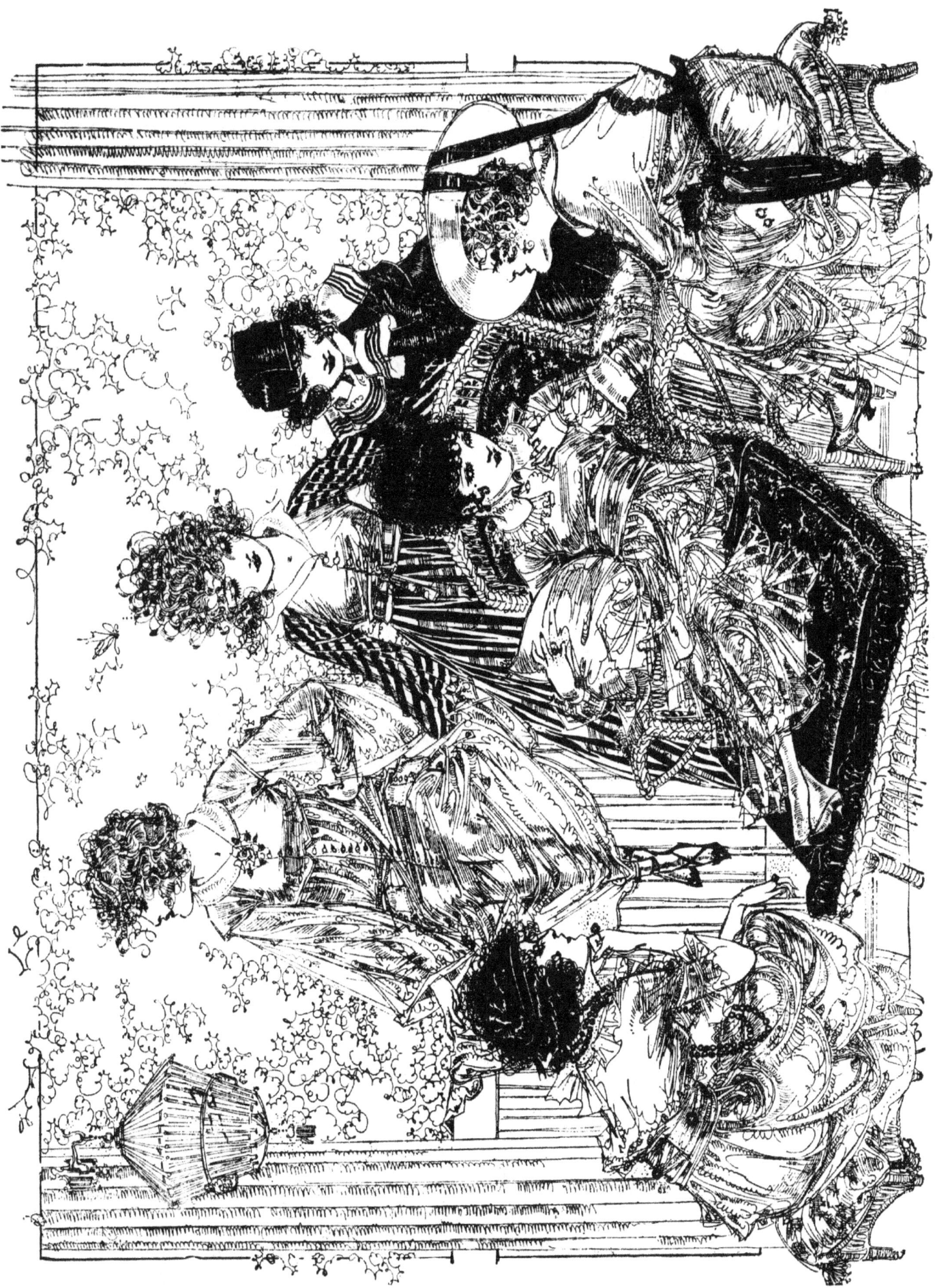

ABOUT THE ILLUSTRATION ON THE REVERSE

Original publication: The Topeka State Journal (Kansas)

Publication date: August 21, 1915

Title: "Find the Girl Who's in Love With the Man They Are Talking About"

Artist: Nell Brinkley

© Copyright 2015 by Synchronista LLC & ClickAmericana.com

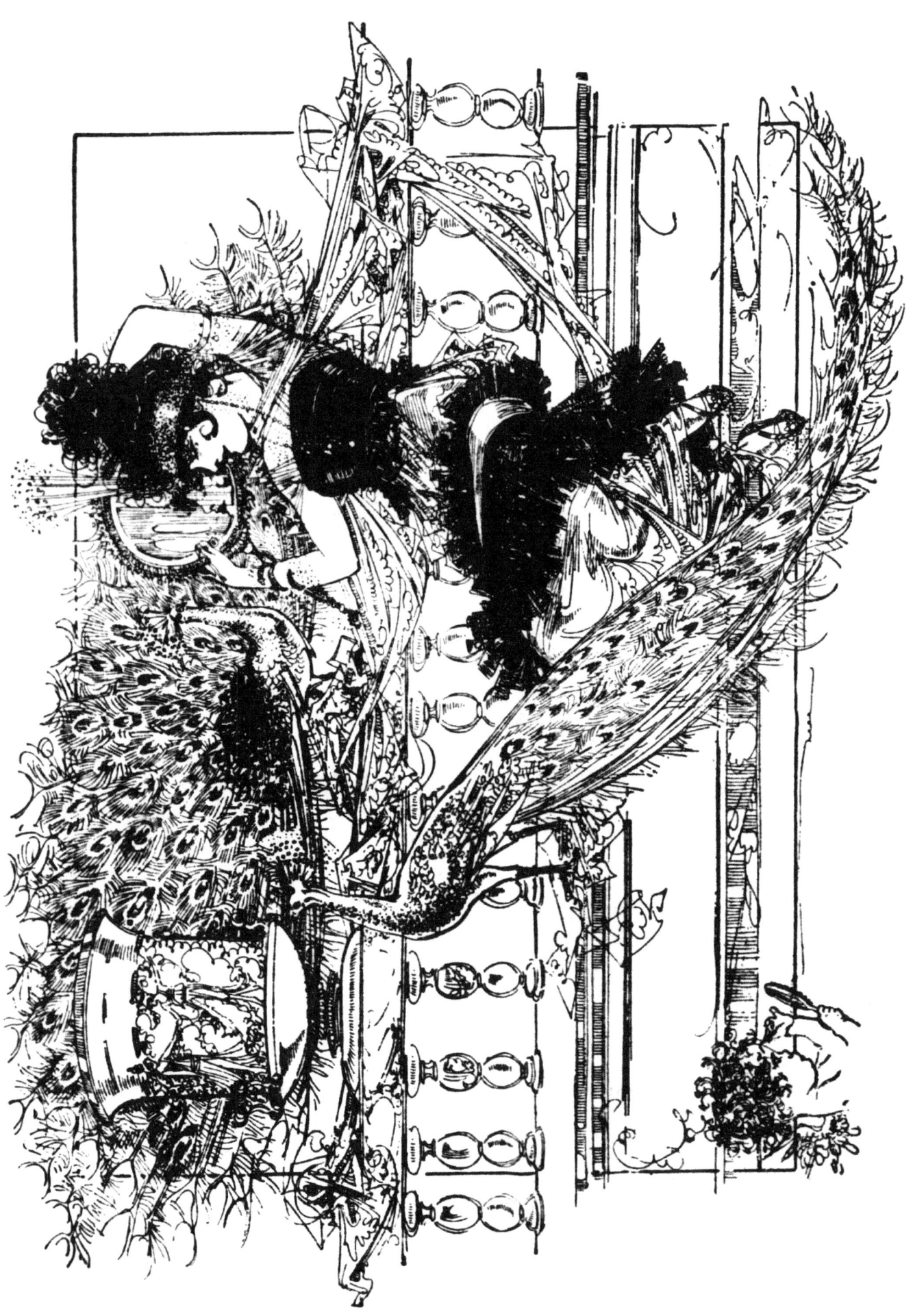

ABOUT THE ILLUSTRATION ON THE REVERSE

Original publication: Omaha Daily Bee (Nebraska)

Publication date: August 10, 1914

Title: "Birds of a Feather"

Artist: Nell Brinkley

© Copyright 2015 by Synchronista LLC & ClickAmericana.com

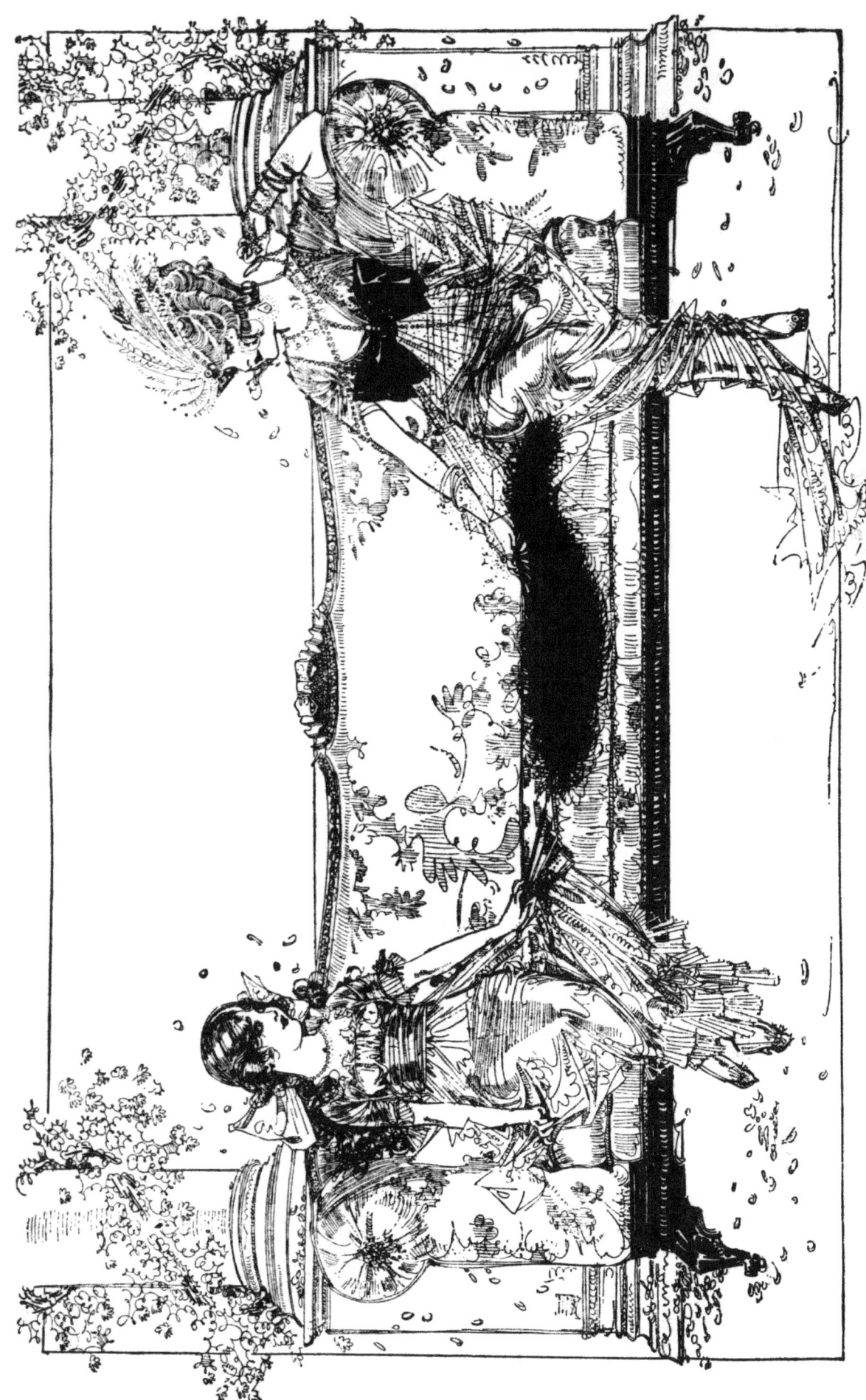

ABOUT THE ILLUSTRATION ON THE REVERSE

Original publication: Omaha Daily Bee (Nebraska)

Publication date: January 24, 1914

Title: "Here is Envy"

Artist: Nell Brinkley

© Copyright 2015 by Synchronista LLC & ClickAmericana.com

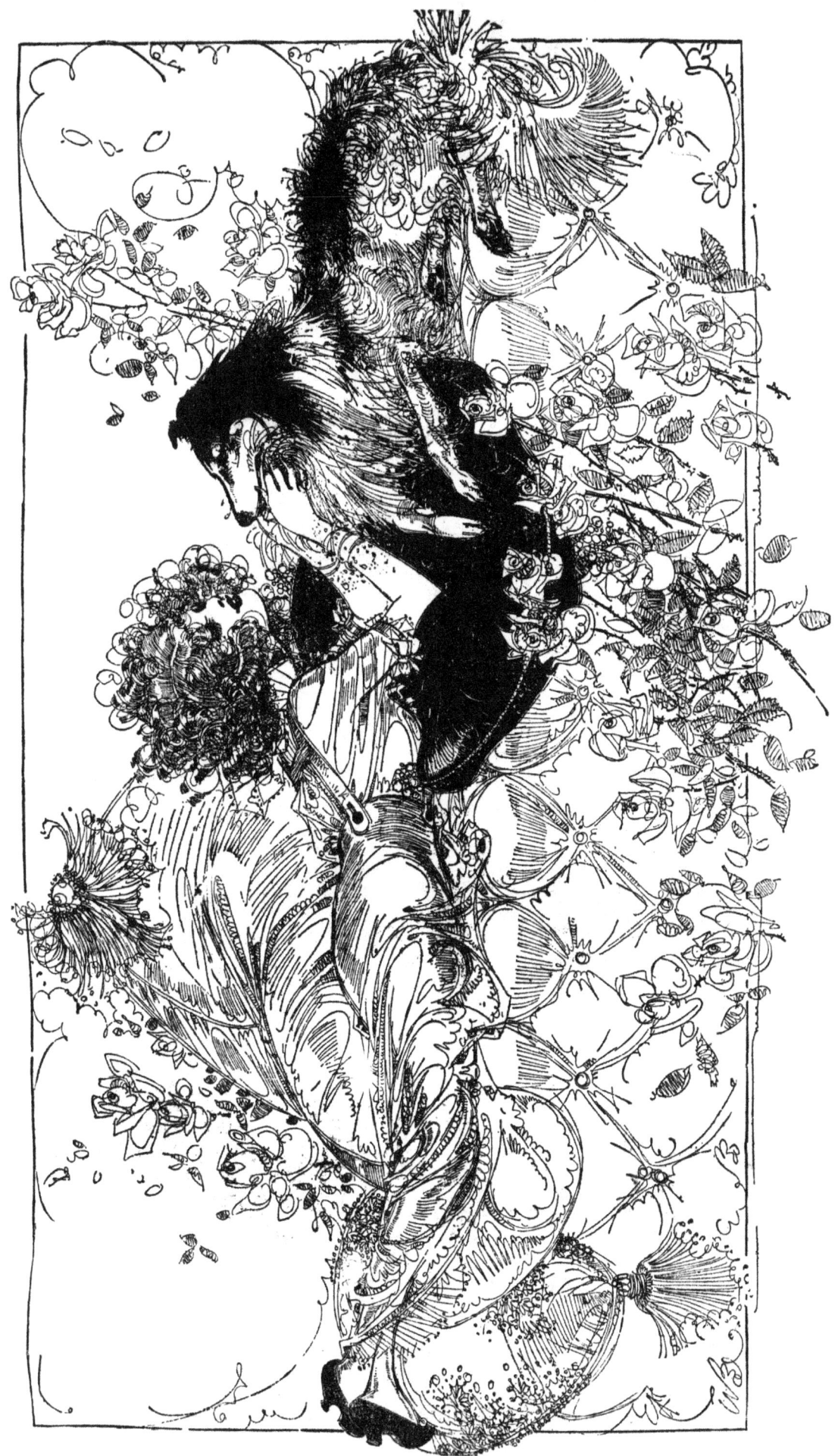

ABOUT THE ILLUSTRATION ON THE REVERSE

Original publication: El Paso Herald (Texas)

Publication date: February 19, 1914

Title: "Beauty and the Beast"

Artist: Nell Brinkley

© Copyright 2015 by Synchronista LLC & ClickAmericana.com

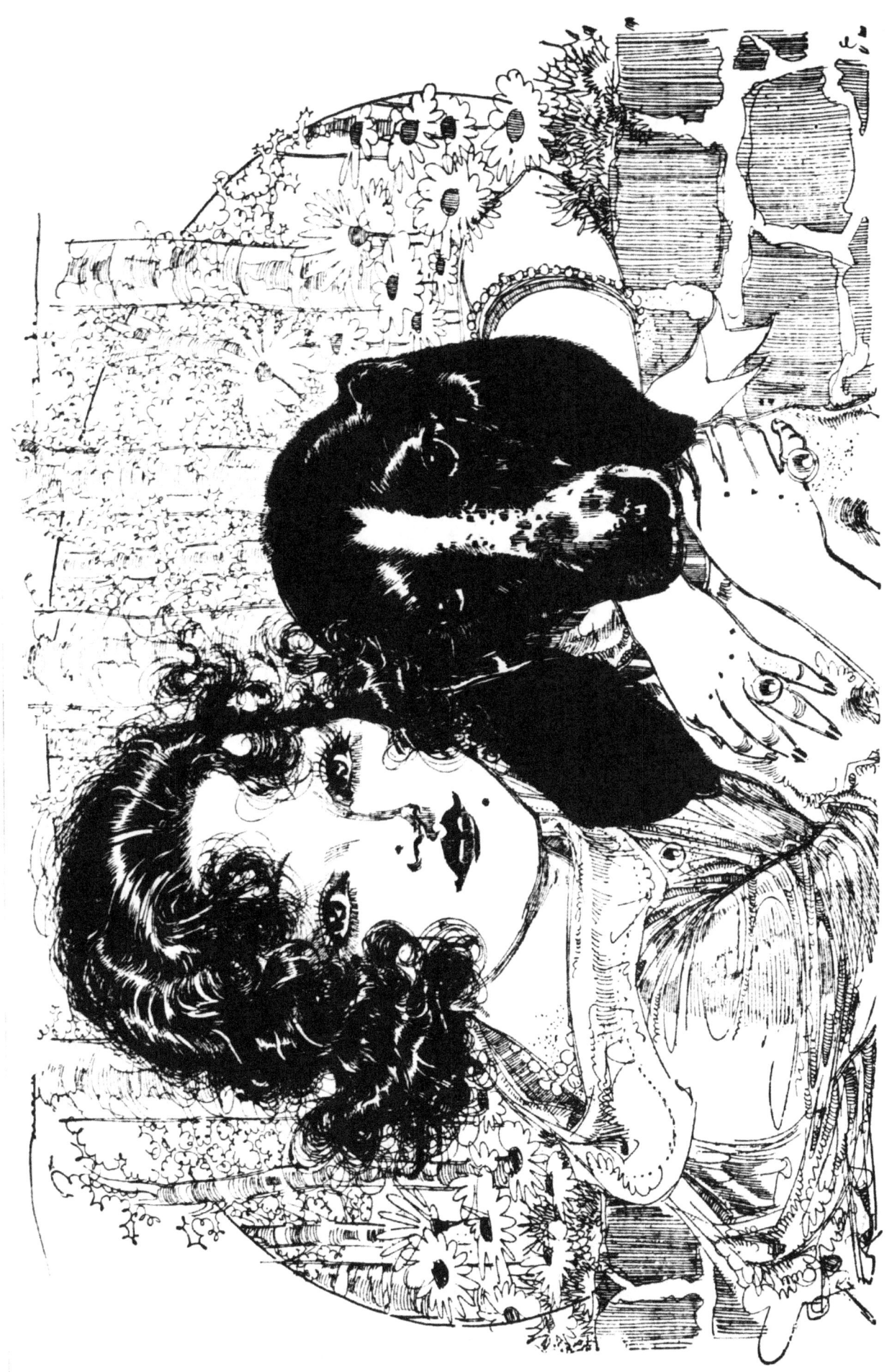

ABOUT THE ILLUSTRATION ON THE REVERSE

Original publication: Omaha Daily Bee (Nebraska)

Publication date: July 14, 1915

Title: "Blue-Ribbon Winners"

Artist: Nell Brinkley

© Copyright 2015 by Synchronista LLC & ClickAmericana.com

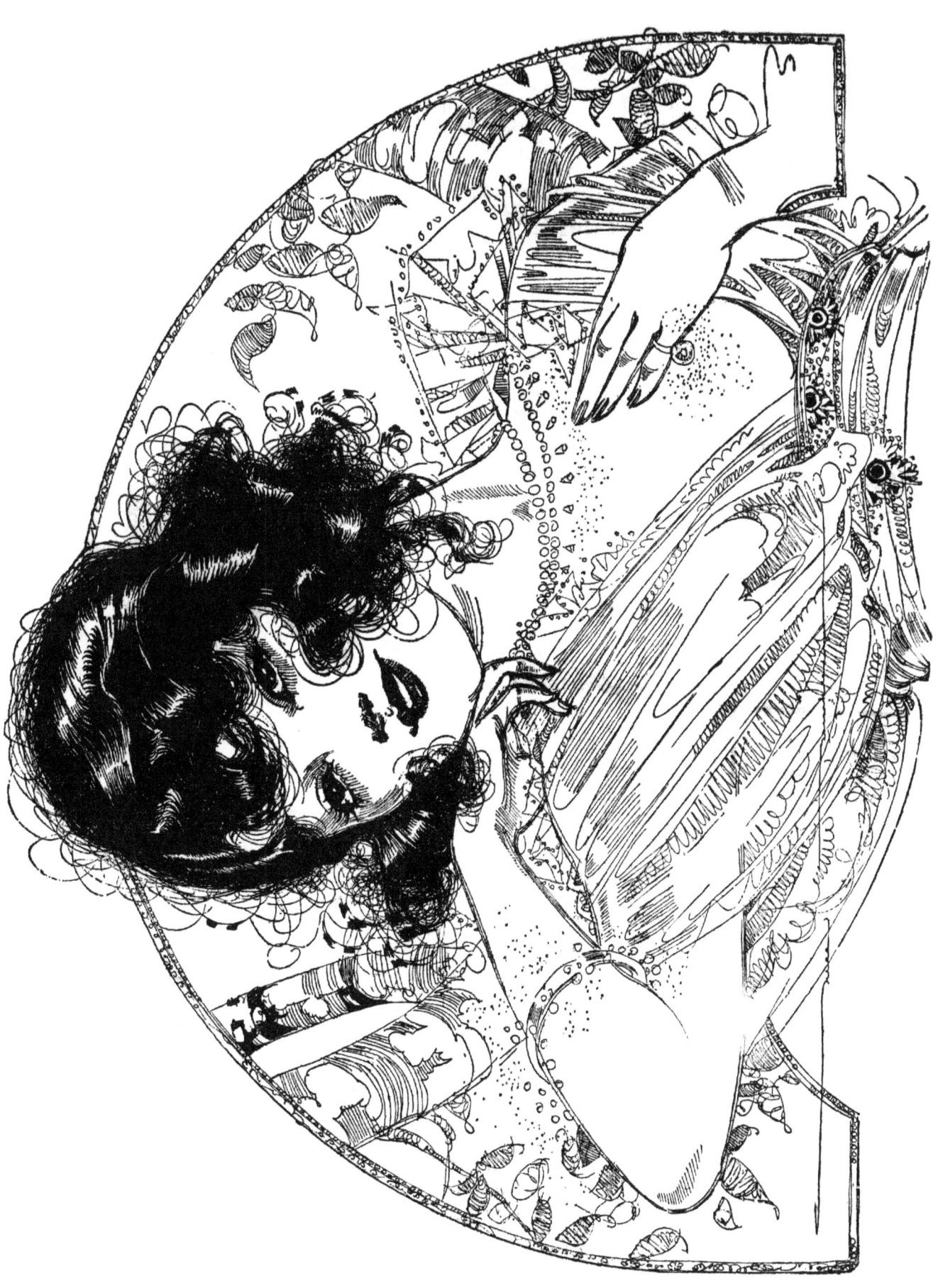

ABOUT THE ILLUSTRATION ON THE REVERSE

Original publication: El Paso Herald (Texas)
Publication date: January 17, 1914
Title: "Mlle. Brown Hair"
Artist: Nell Brinkley

© Copyright 2015 by Synchronista LLC & ClickAmericana.com

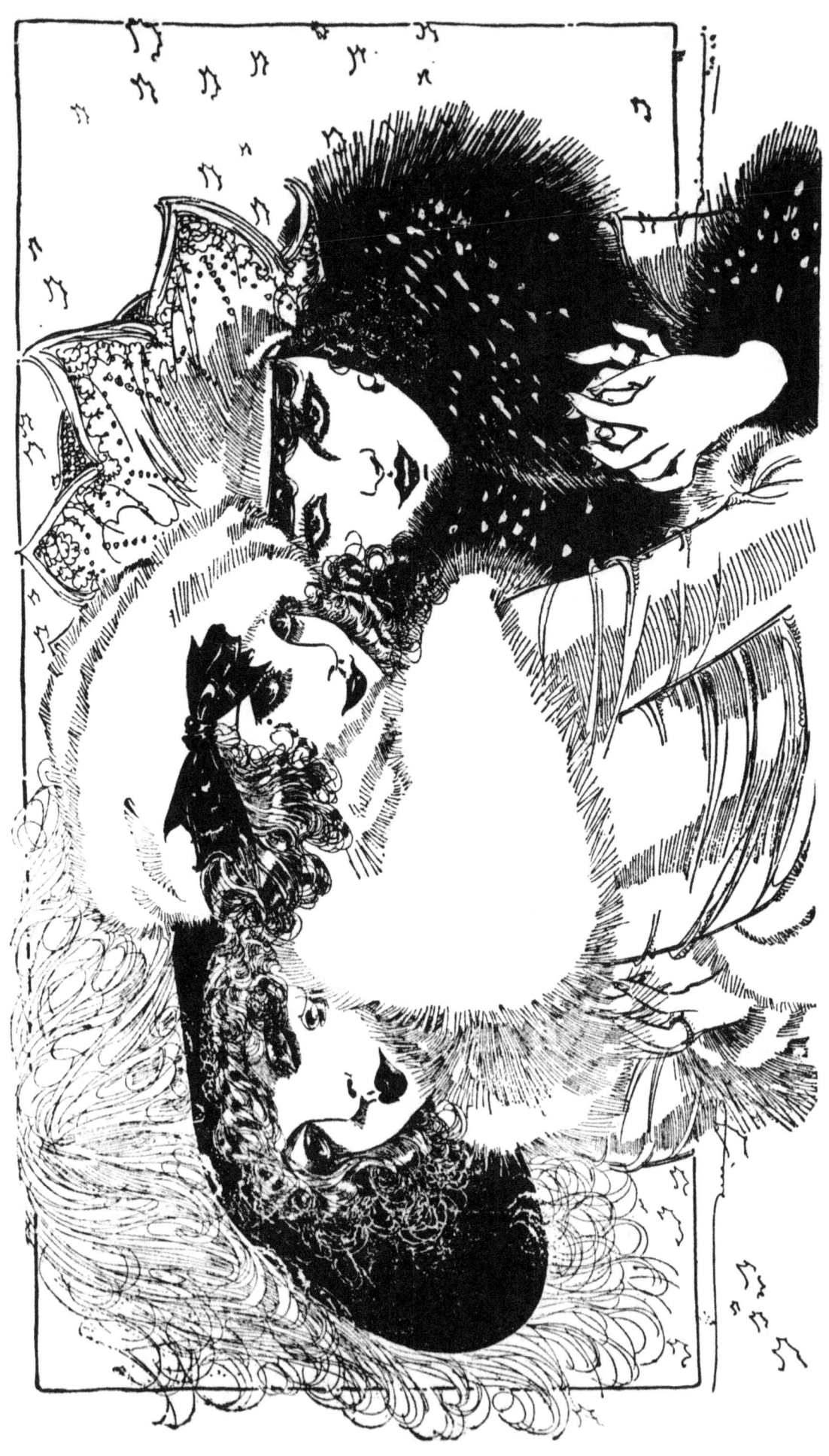

ABOUT THE ILLUSTRATION ON THE REVERSE

Original publication: The Washington Times (DC)

Publication date: December 22, 1919

Title: "'Killing' Looks"

Artist: Nell Brinkley

© Copyright 2015 by Synchronista LLC & ClickAmericana.com

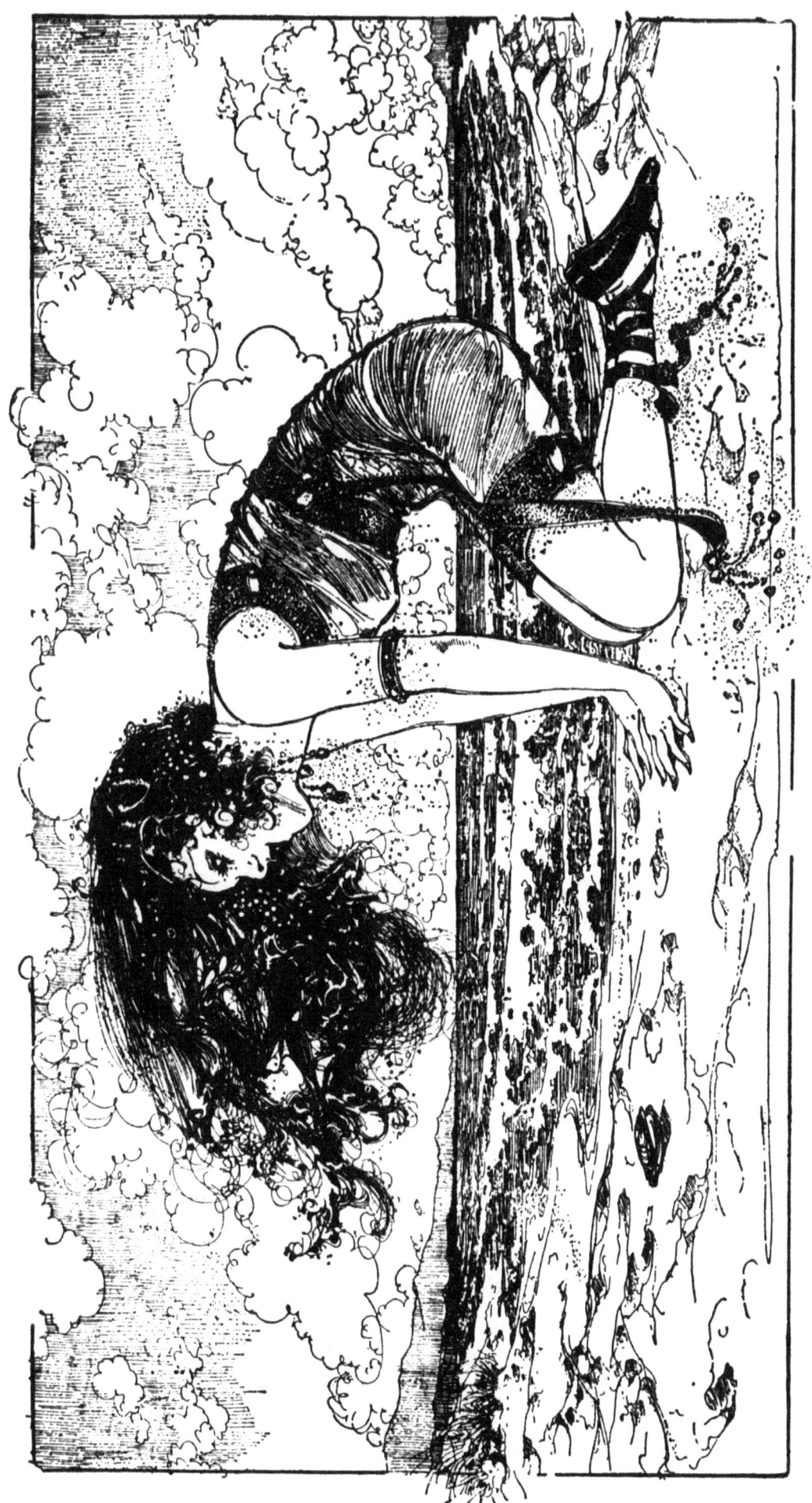

ABOUT THE ILLUSTRATION ON THE REVERSE

Original publication: The Washington Times (DC)

Publication date: August 30, 1917

Title: "A Born Flirt"

Artist: Nell Brinkley

© Copyright 2015 by Synchronista LLC & ClickAmericana.com

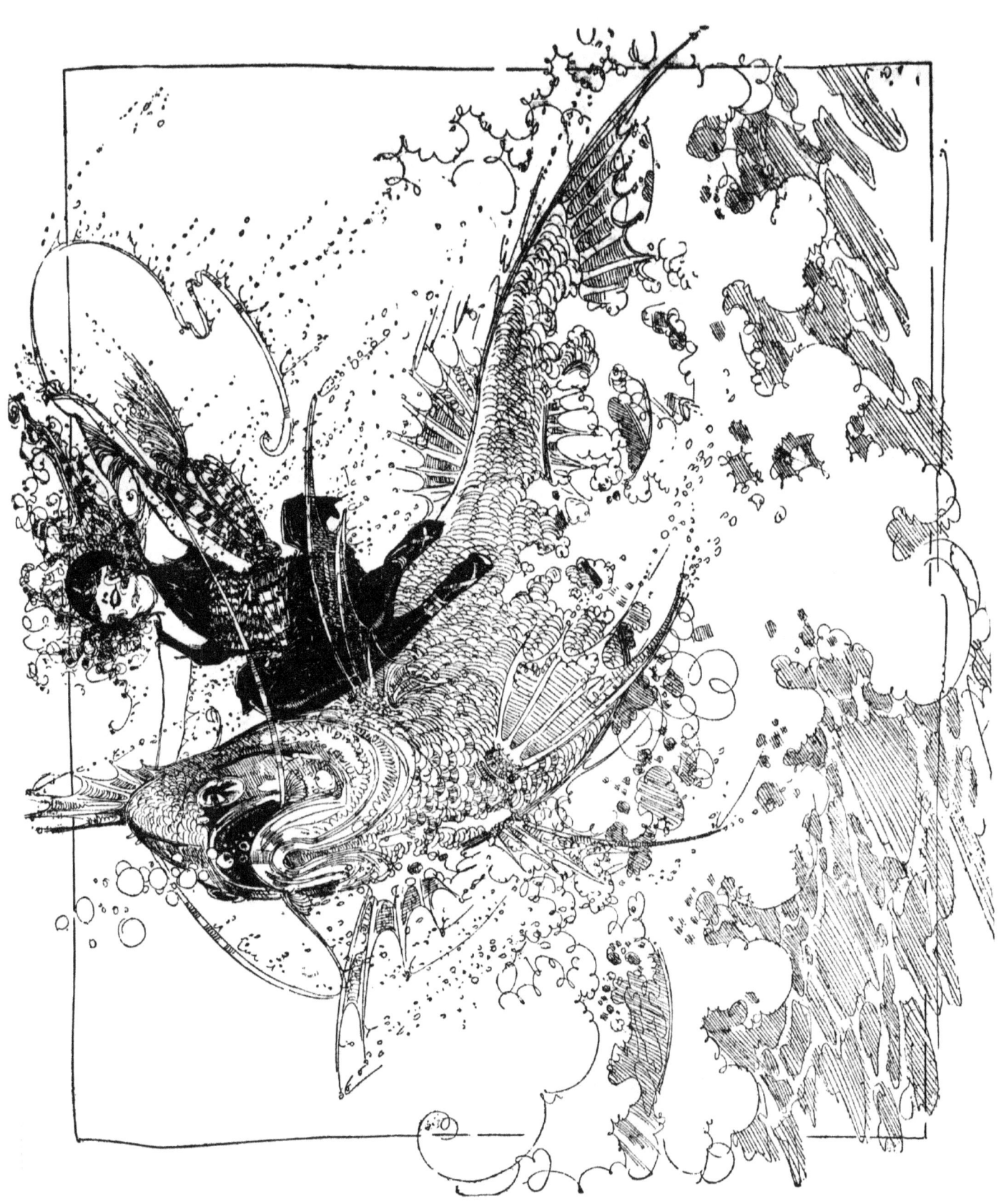

ABOUT THE ILLUSTRATION ON THE REVERSE

Original publication: El Paso Herald (Texas)

Publication date: May 16, 1914

Title: "COMING!"

Artist: Nell Brinkley

© Copyright 2015 by Synchronista LLC & ClickAmericana.com

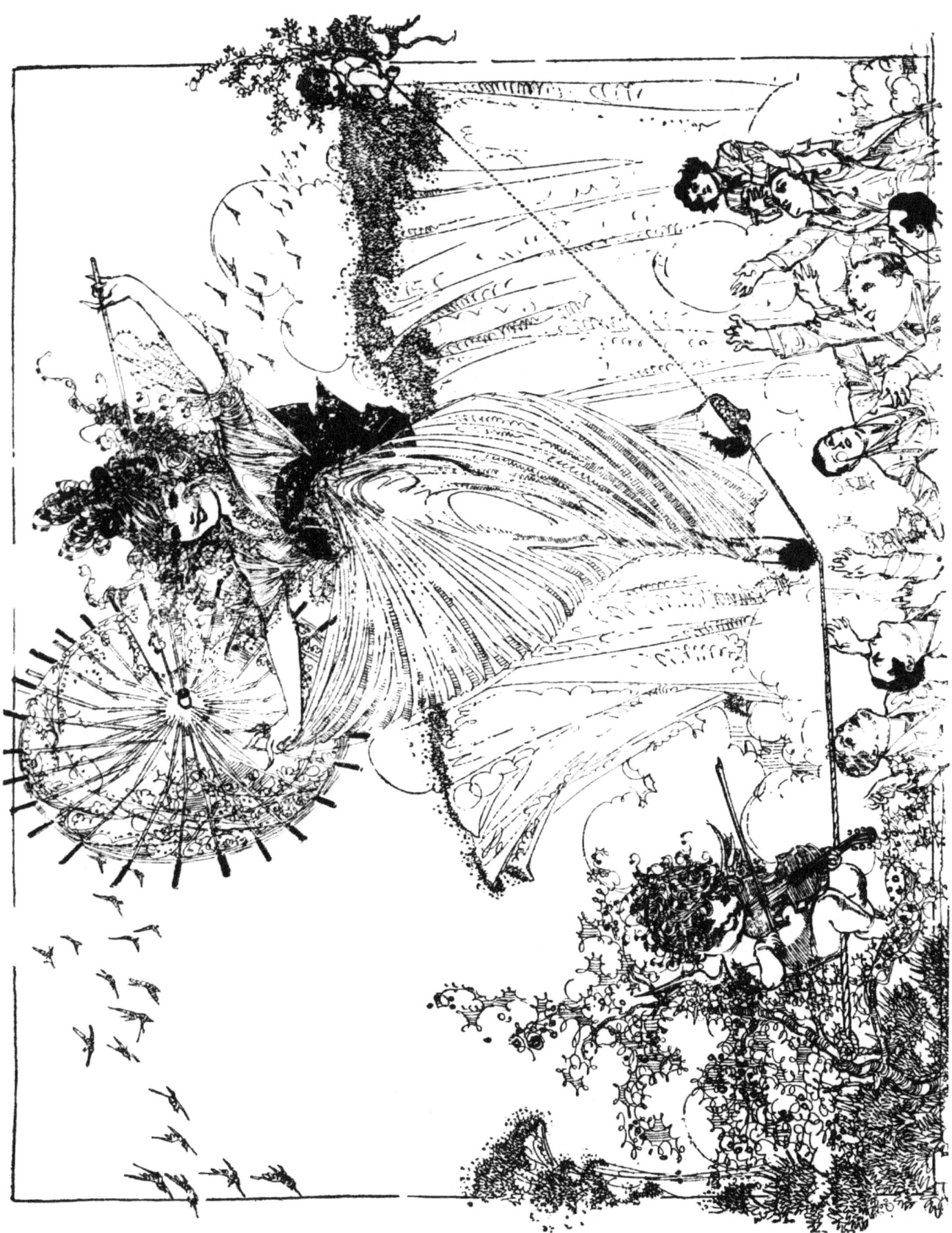

ABOUT THE ILLUSTRATION ON THE REVERSE

Original publication: Omaha Daily Bee (Nebraska)

Publication date: June 04, 1914

Title: "Being Eighteen"

Artist: Nell Brinkley

© Copyright 2015 by Synchronista LLC & ClickAmericana.com

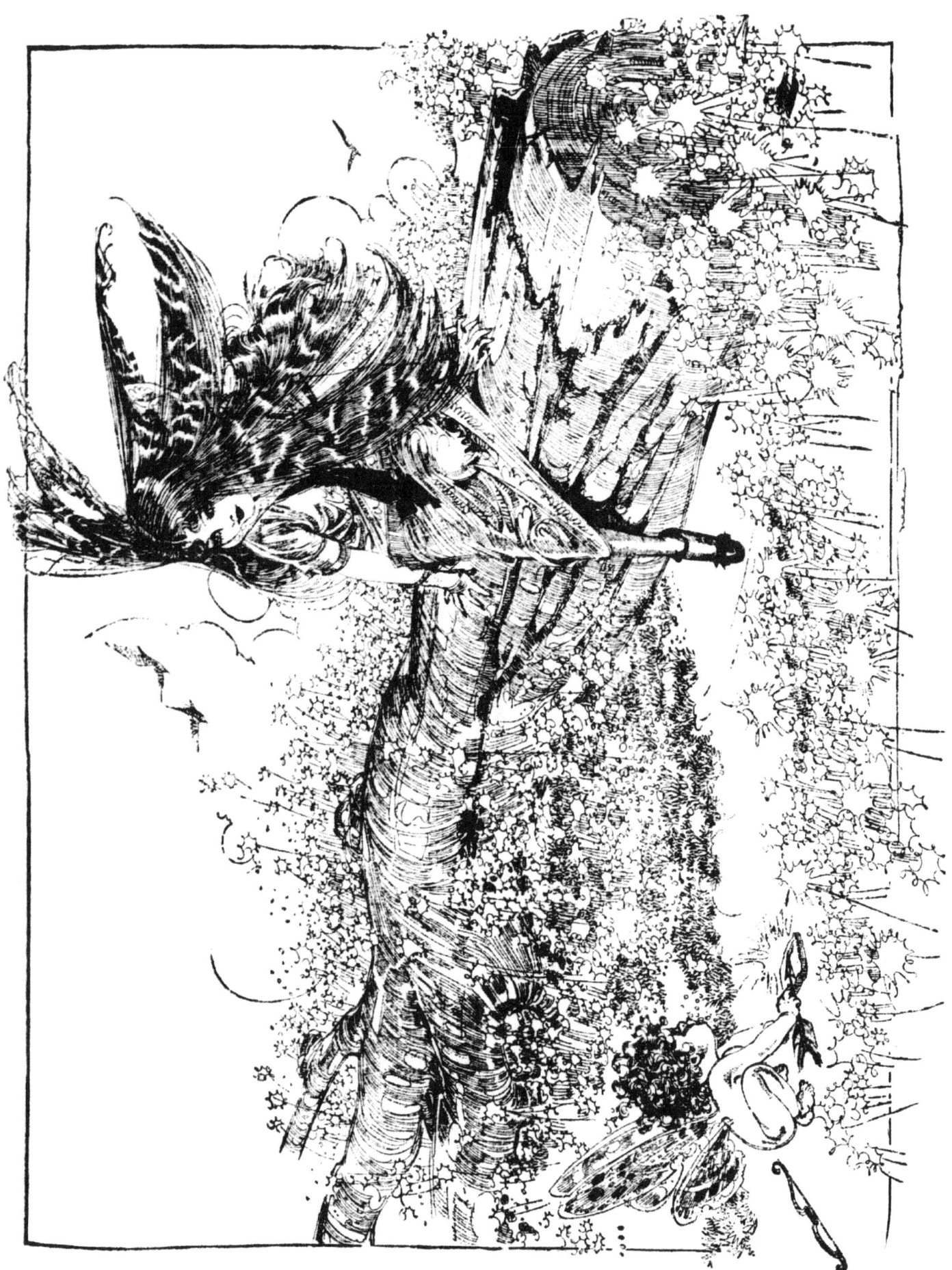

ABOUT THE ILLUSTRATION ON THE REVERSE

Original publication: Omaha Daily Bee (Nebraska)

Publication date: August 28, 1914

Title: "I'm Sharpening This for You"

Artist: Nell Brinkley

© Copyright 2015 by Synchronista LLC & ClickAmericana.com

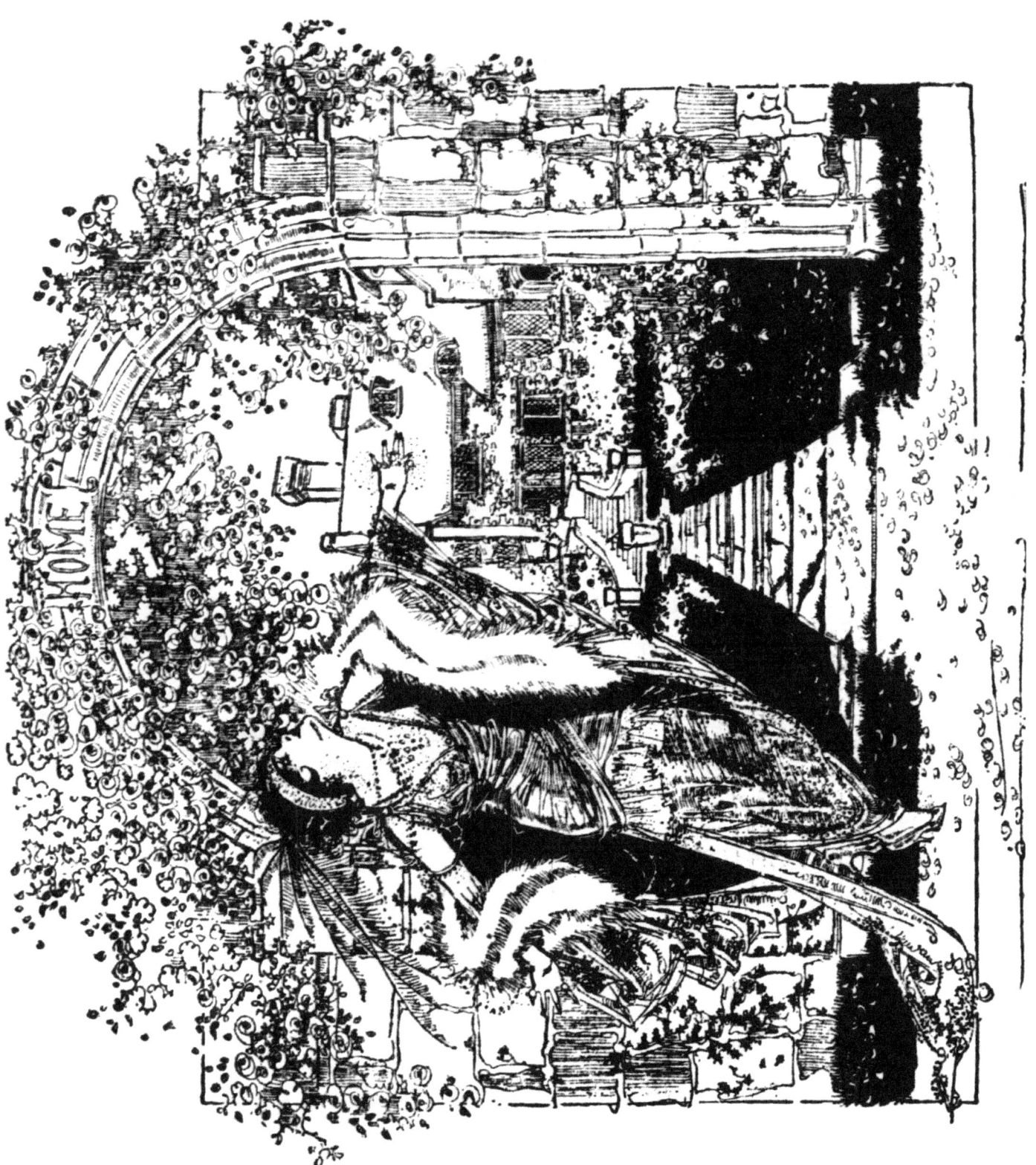

ABOUT THE ILLUSTRATION ON THE REVERSE

Original publication: Omaha Daily Bee (Nebraska)

Publication date: April 13, 1915

Title: "A World Within a World"

Artist: Nell Brinkley

© Copyright 2015 by Synchronista LLC & ClickAmericana.com

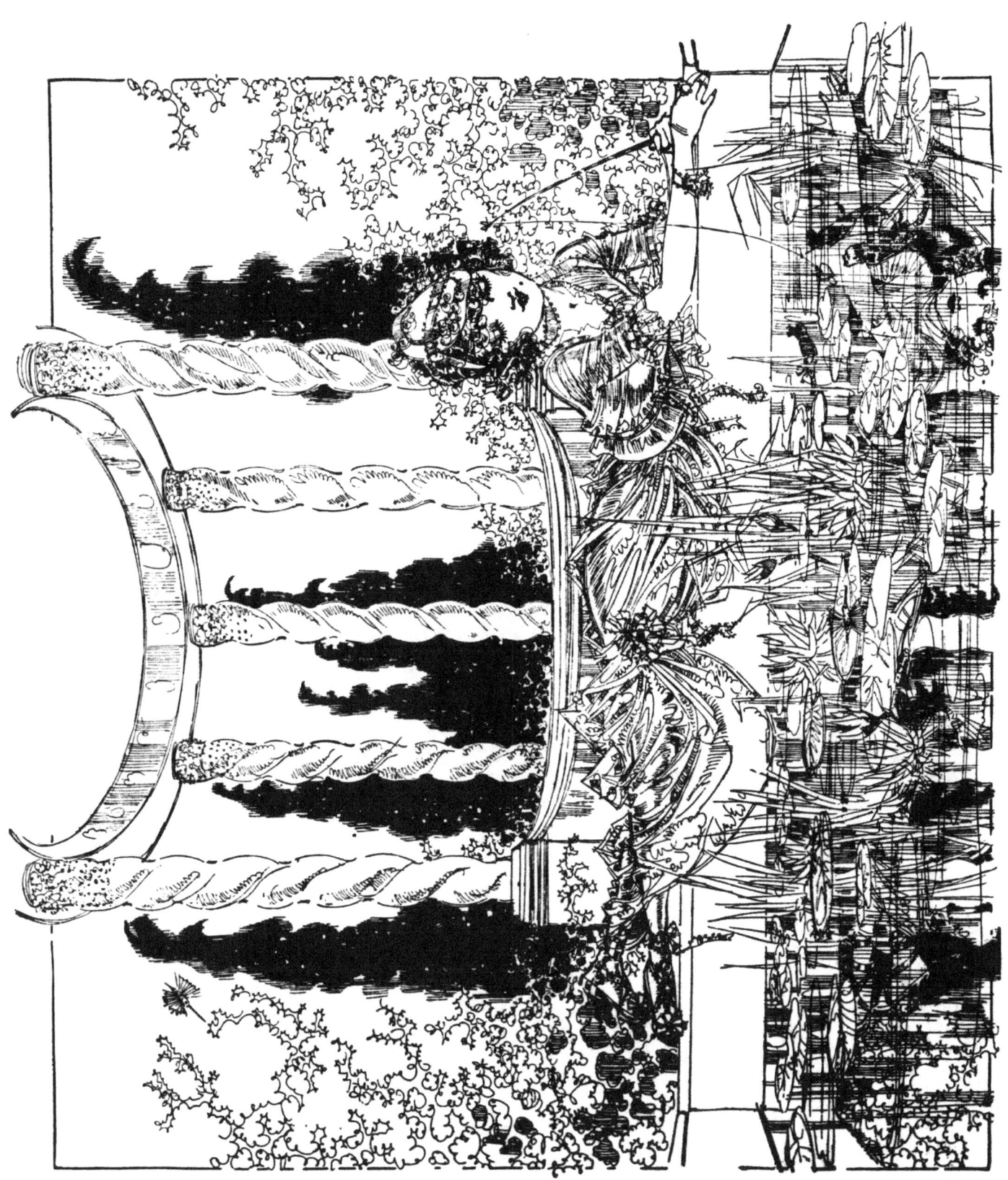

ABOUT THE ILLUSTRATION ON THE REVERSE

Original publication: Omaha Daily Bee (Nebraska)

Publication date: September 13, 1915

Title: "Good Fishing Weather"

Artist: Nell Brinkley

© Copyright 2015 by Synchronista LLC & ClickAmericana.com

The End

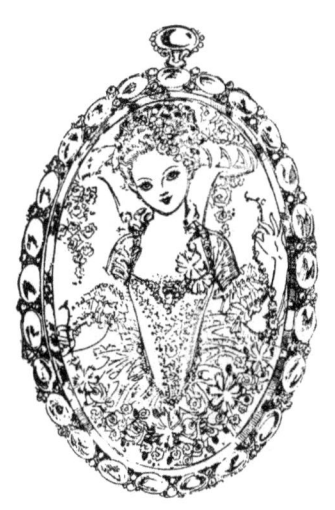

About the artist

NELL BRINKLEY (1886-1944)

One of America's most popular but forgotten artists, Nell Brinkley, was born just outside of Denver, Colorado, on September 5, 1886.

By age 17, the girl already knew what she wanted to do with her life, and left high school to become an artist. But it wasn't until she was 21 years old that she got her big break, when newspaper magnate William Randolph Hearst invited her to create illustrations for his paper, the *New York Evening Journal*.

But she was more than an artist with pen and ink: Fanciful observations accompanied many of her pieces, and also helped to reflect the beauty, fashion and trends of the era.

She was so successful that by 1908, the young woman was well on her way to becoming a household name, with stores nationwide offering "Nell Brinkley styles" of suits, coats and hats. Soon came popular songs, stage shows — and even the inclusion of the "Brinkley Girls" in the famous Ziegfeld Follies theatrical productions.

In 1925, one of her peers, American journalist Jack Lait, wrote the following in a syndicated newspaper article about Brinkley's life and work:

Sentiments such as Nell writes — saccharine, bubbling, often fulsome — from anyone else would be ludicrous or depressing. From her they are joy-radiating. She can simper, she can sniffle, she can effuse, she can even rave; but she has that faculty for making us fall into her mood, often a mood into which we, mundane parties, never otherwise slip. Her drawings register the same amazing qualities. Whether we like fluffy, tiptilt-nosed hoydens, chubby cupids and collar-ad heroes or not — and I don't — we adore them when Nell draws them.

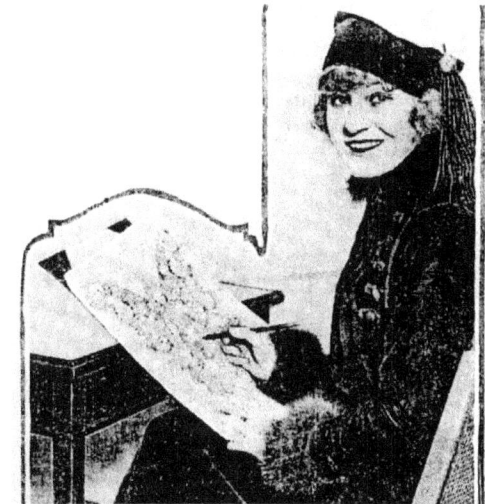

Above: Nell Brinkley, as featured in the *San Francisco Call and Post* on August 31, 1915. She can be seen working on "The Last of Summer" — the butterfly image on this book's cover.

Brinkley's career flourished for more than a quarter century, but demand for her services waned in 1935, as illustrations began to be phased out in favor of photographs.

Despite her obvious affection for romance and family, she left this world in 1944 — divorced and estranged from her only child. With the world in the throes of World War II, her death merited but a few lines in the back pages of the newspapers whose pages she had once decorated.

We hope that this book will help reintroduce Nell Brinkley's timeless work to a whole new generation.

Like this book?
Check out our websites, too!

ClickAmericana.com
Thousands of articles, photos and vintage ads
from throughout American history.

PrintColorFun.com
Hundreds of free coloring pages
to download and print at home.

Myria.com
Smart stuff for real life:
Health, parenting, psychology,
science, tech, entertainment — plus
recipes, home decor & other good things.

www.ingramcontent.com/pod-product-compliance
Lightning Source LLC
Chambersburg PA
CBHW080944170526
45158CB00008B/2366